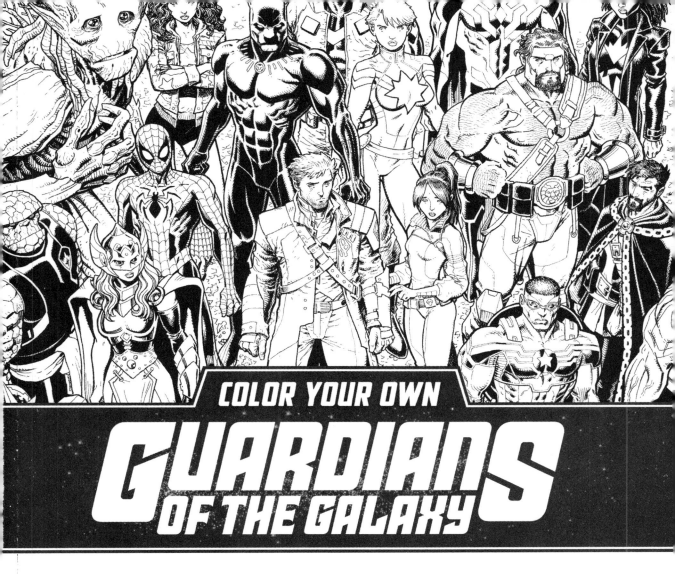

COLOR YOUR OWN GUARDIANS OF THE GALAXY

ARTISTS:

Ed McGuinness, Mark Farmer, Sara Pichelli, Scott Hepburn, Nick Bradshaw, Scott Hanna, Marco Checchetto, Joe Quesada, Danny Miki, Steve McNiven, John Dell, Valerio Schiti, Arthur Adams, Aaron Kuder, Frank Cho, Jim Valentino, Wellinton Alves, Manny Clark, Dexter Vines, Ryan Stegman, Todd Nauck, Brian Kesinger, Jim Cheung, Walden Wong, Guillermo Ortego, Mike Mayhew, Skottie Young, Brett Bean, Paco Medina, Juan Vlasco & Javier Garrón

- - - ◻ - - -

COLLECTION EDITOR: Jennifer Grünwald
ASSISTANT EDITOR: Caitlin O'Connell
ASSOCIATE MANAGING EDITOR: Kateri Woody
EDITOR, SPECIAL PROJECTS: Mark D. Beazley

VP PRODUCTION & SPECIAL PROJECTS: Jeff Youngquist
SVP PRINT, SALES & MARKETING: David Gabriel
RESEARCH: Jess Harrold

EDITOR IN CHIEF: Axel Alonso
CHIEF CREATIVE OFFICER: Joe Quesada
Buckley
Alan Fine

D1501884

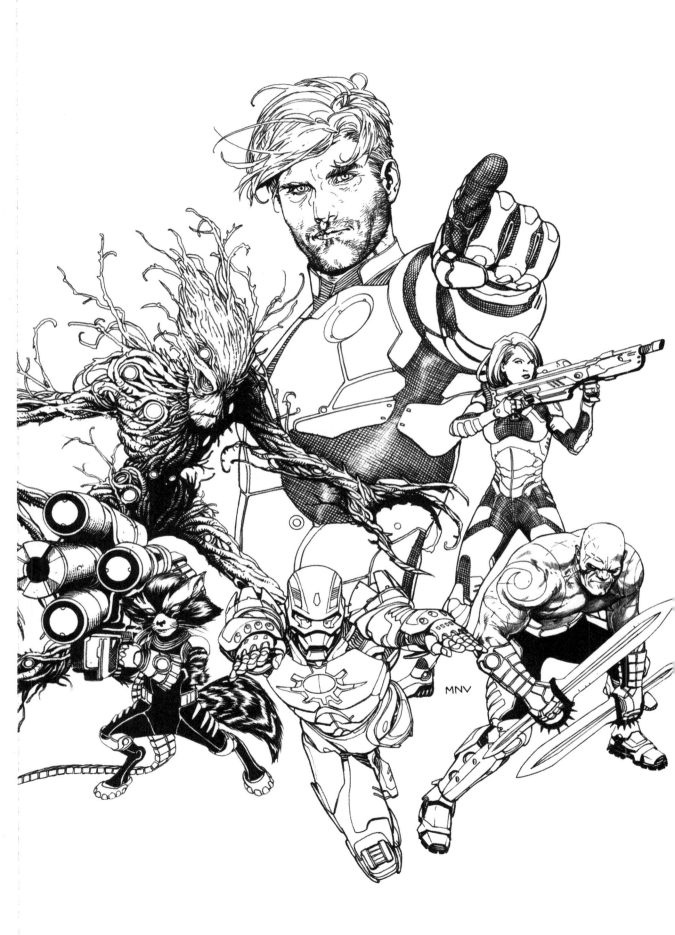

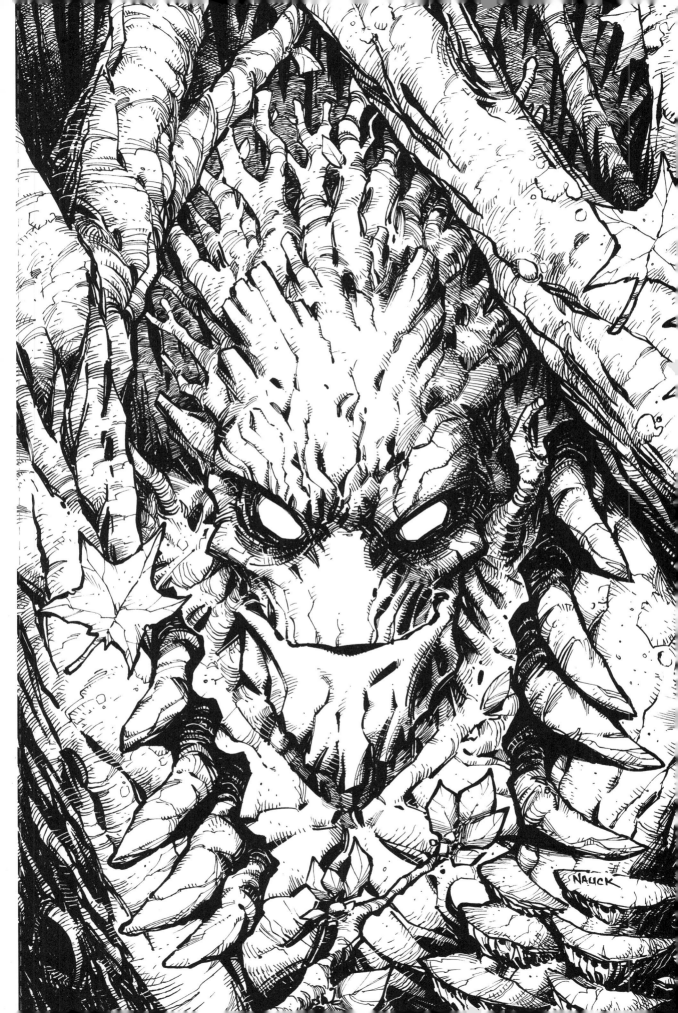

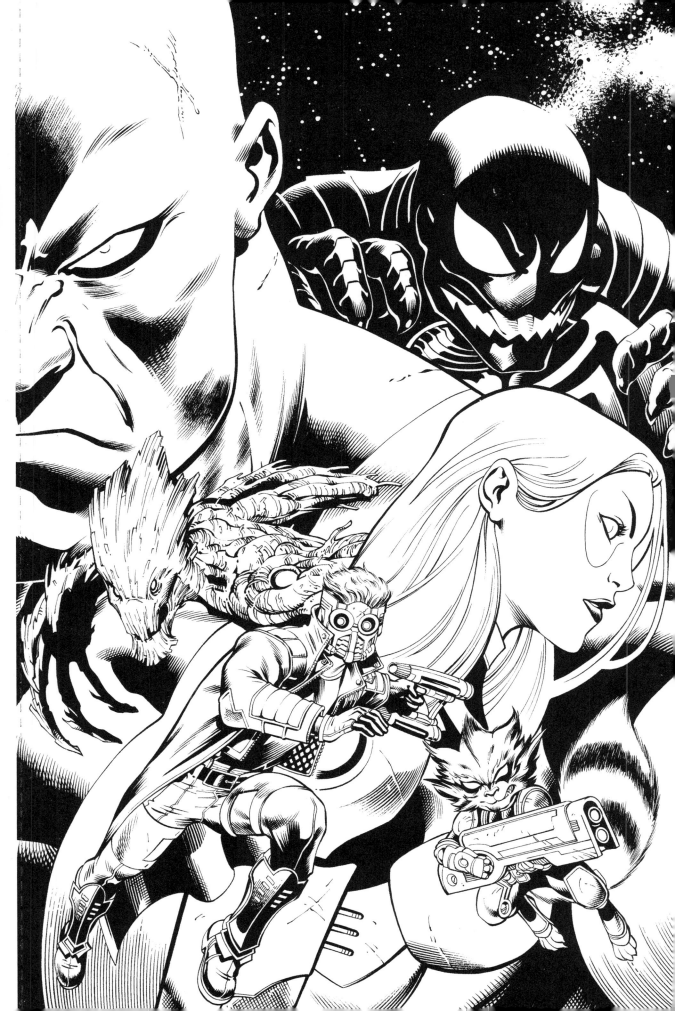

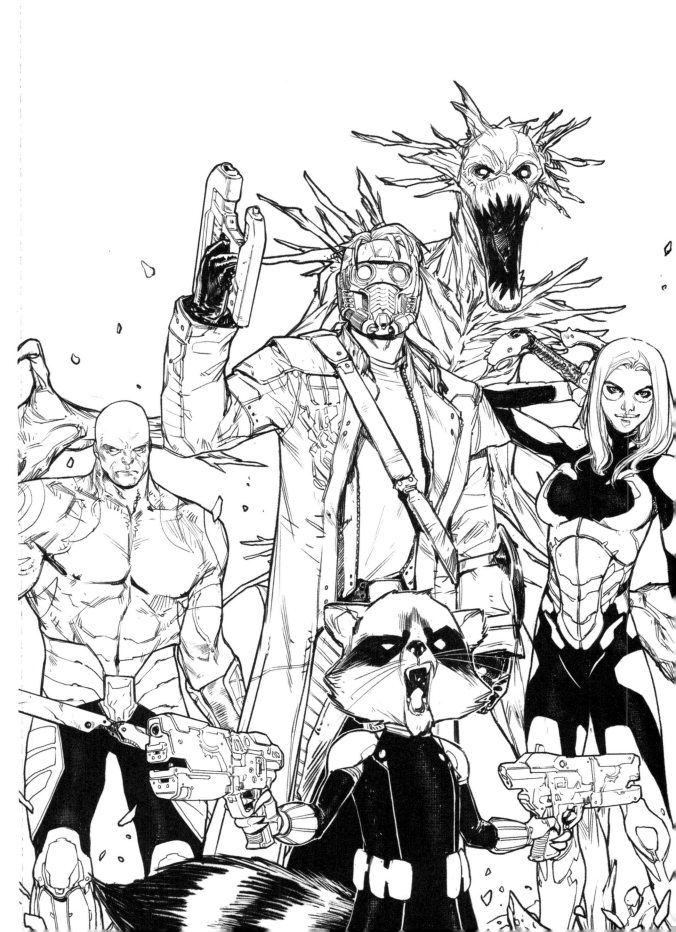

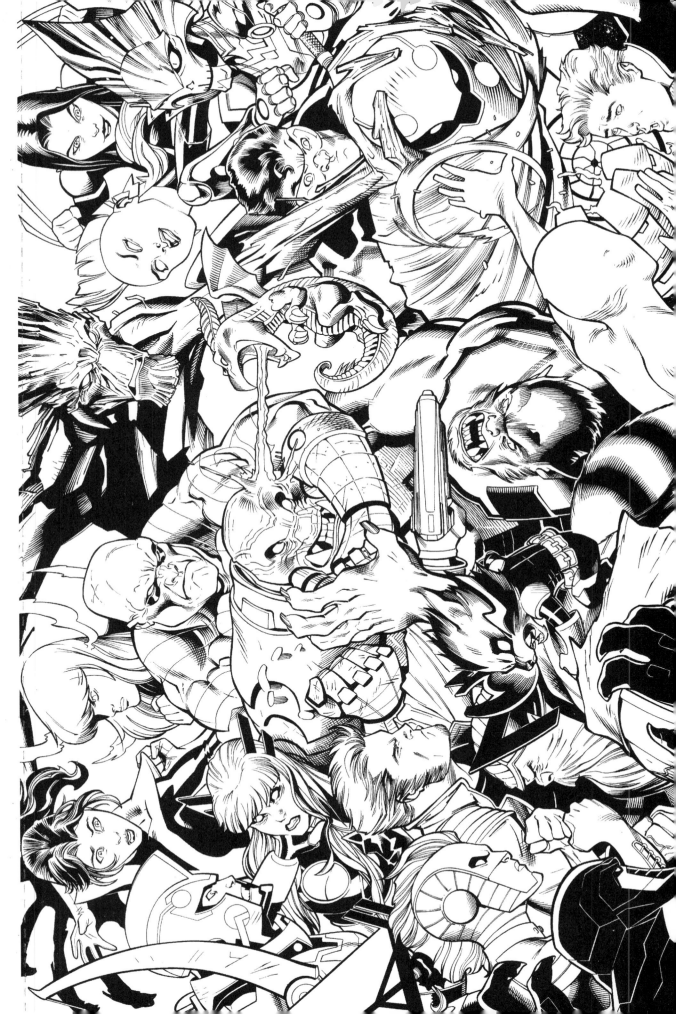

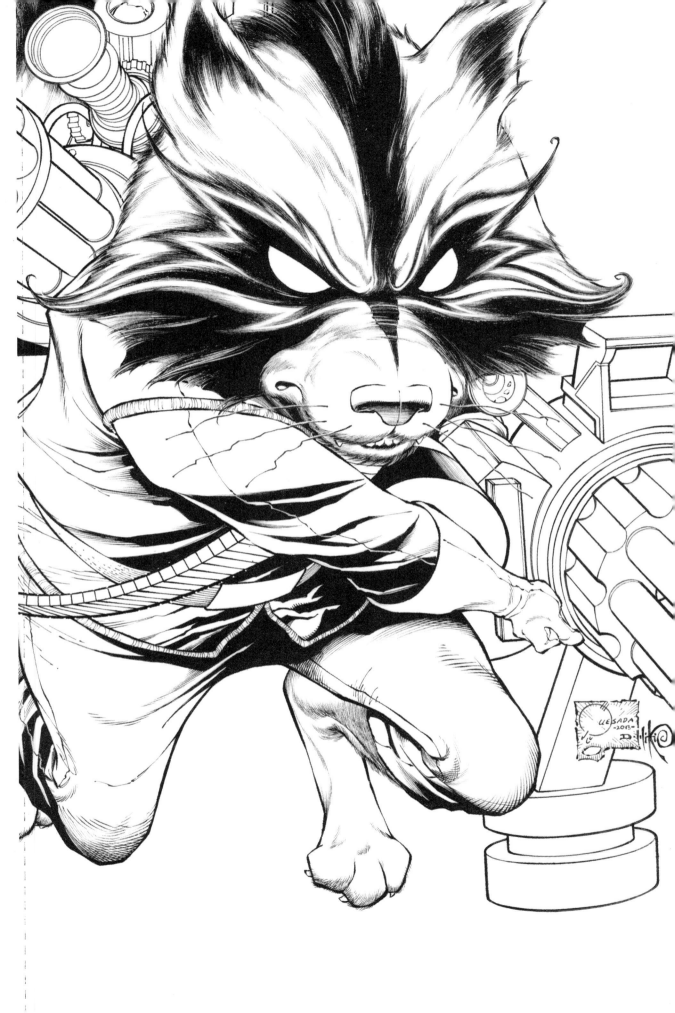

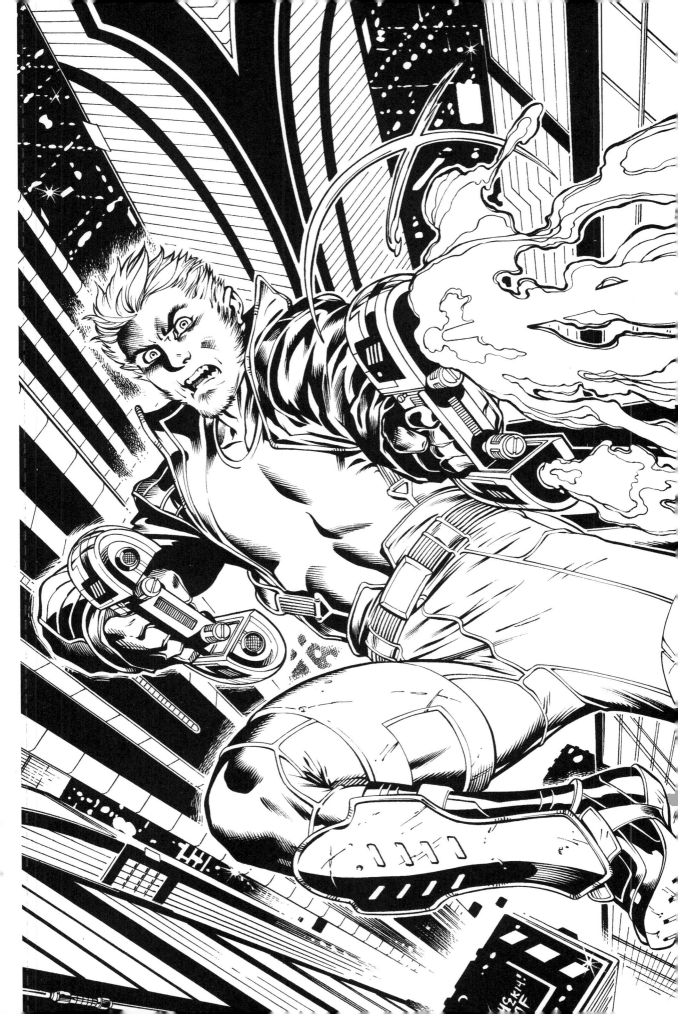

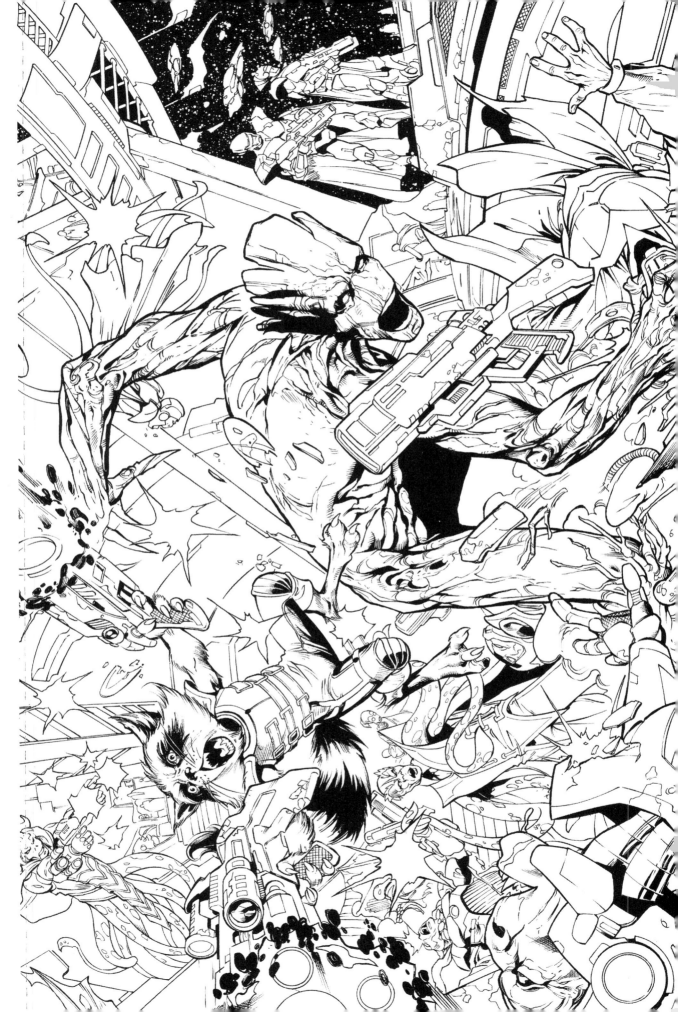

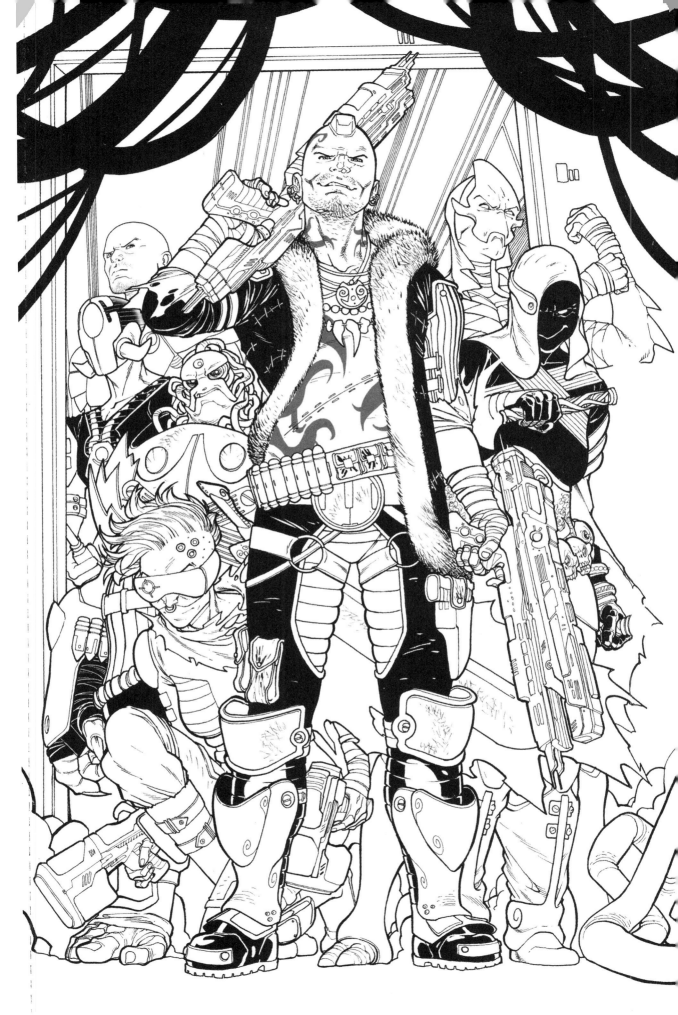

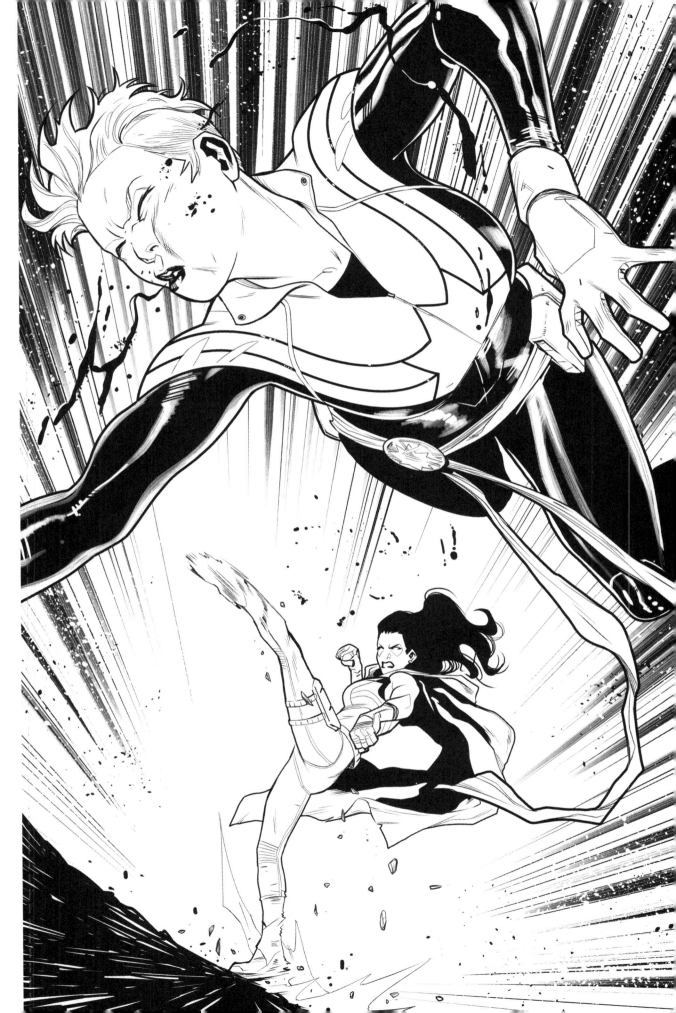

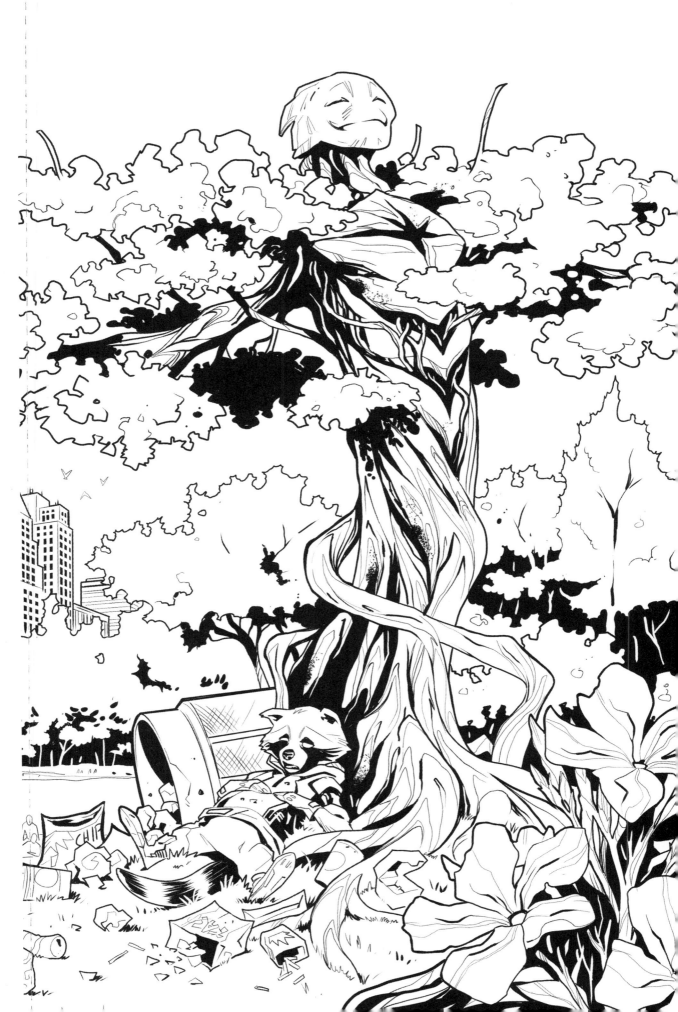

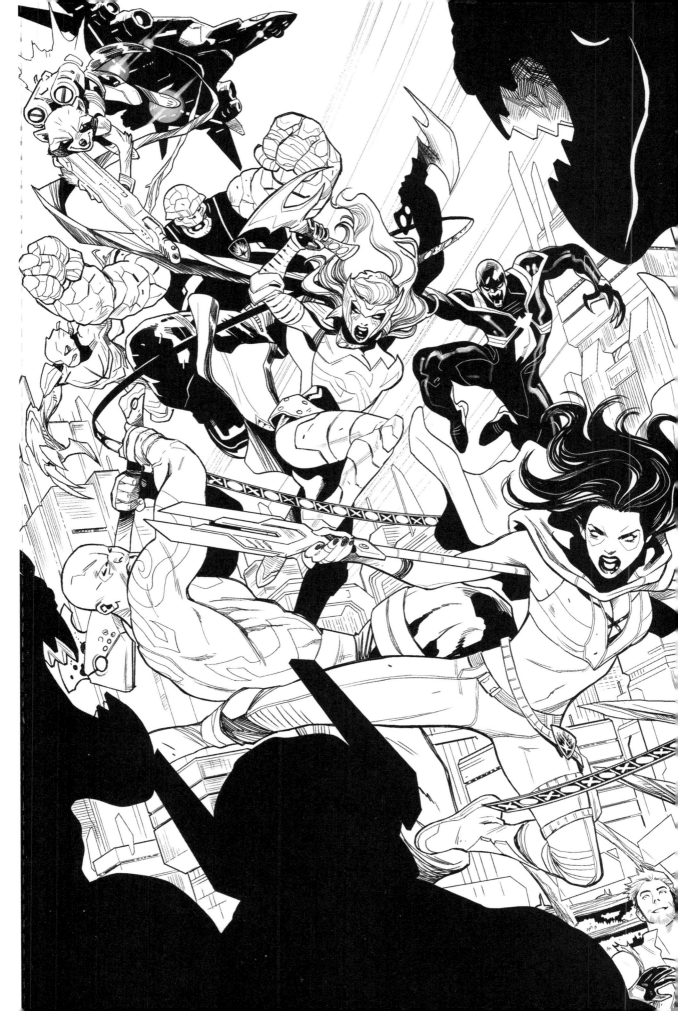

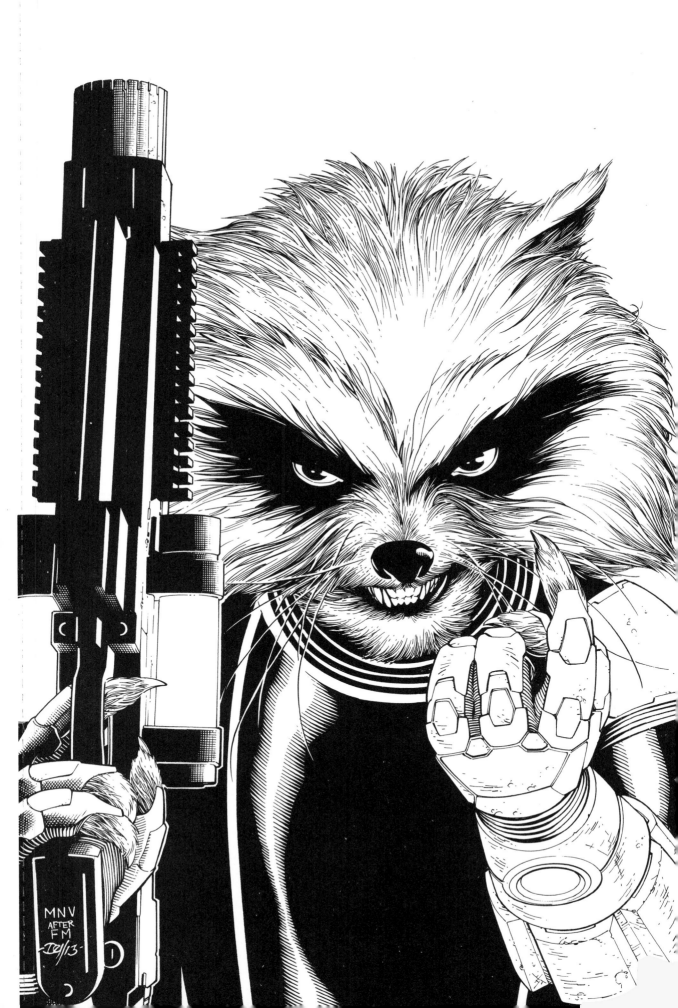

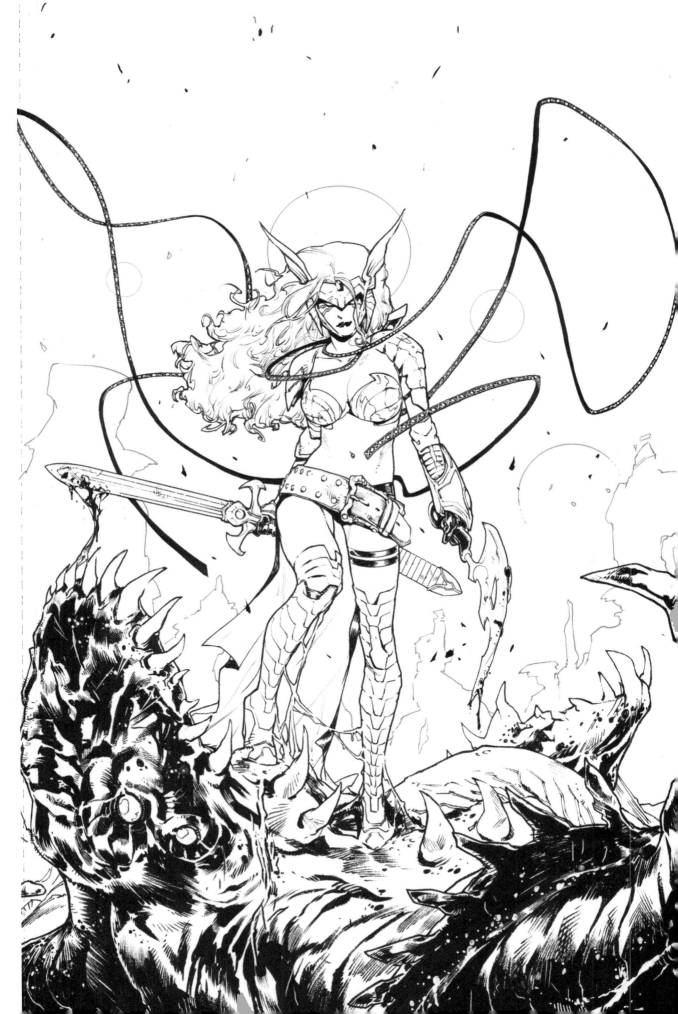

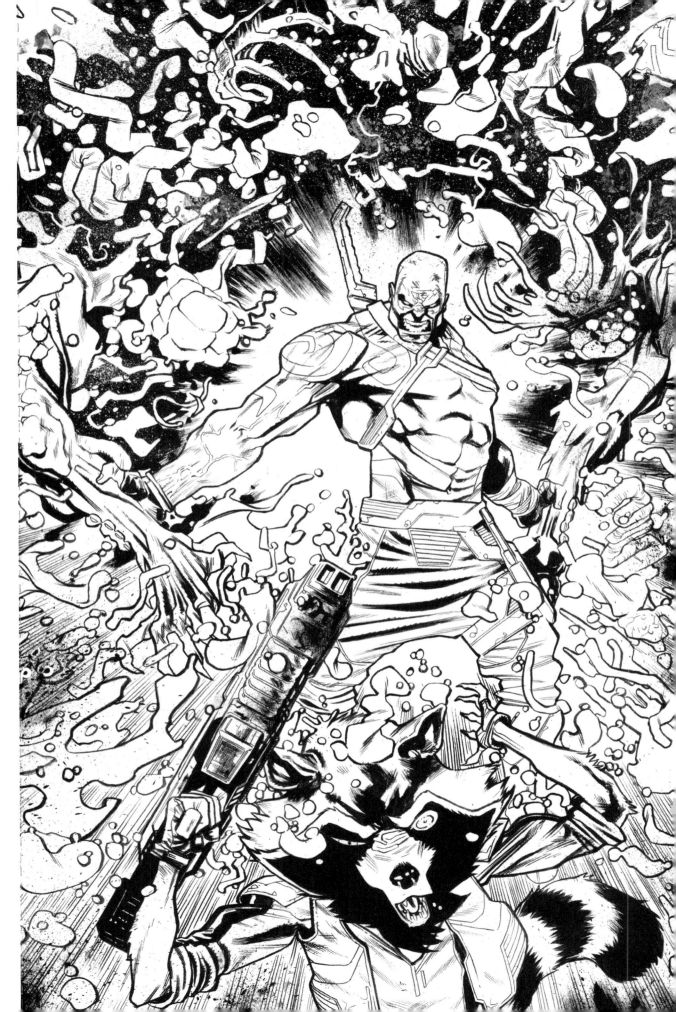

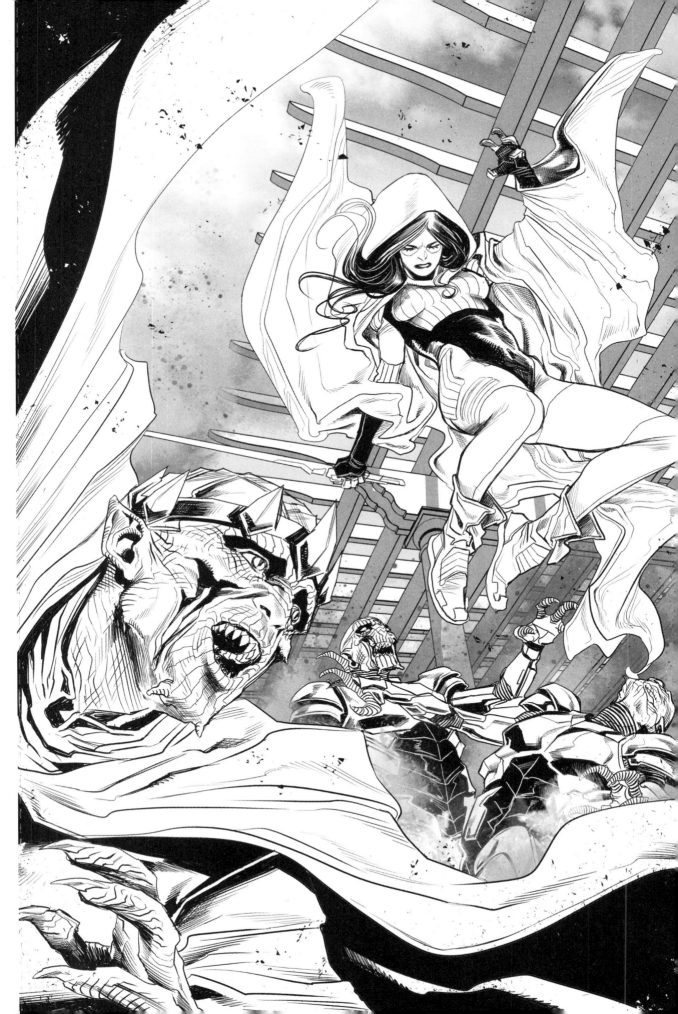

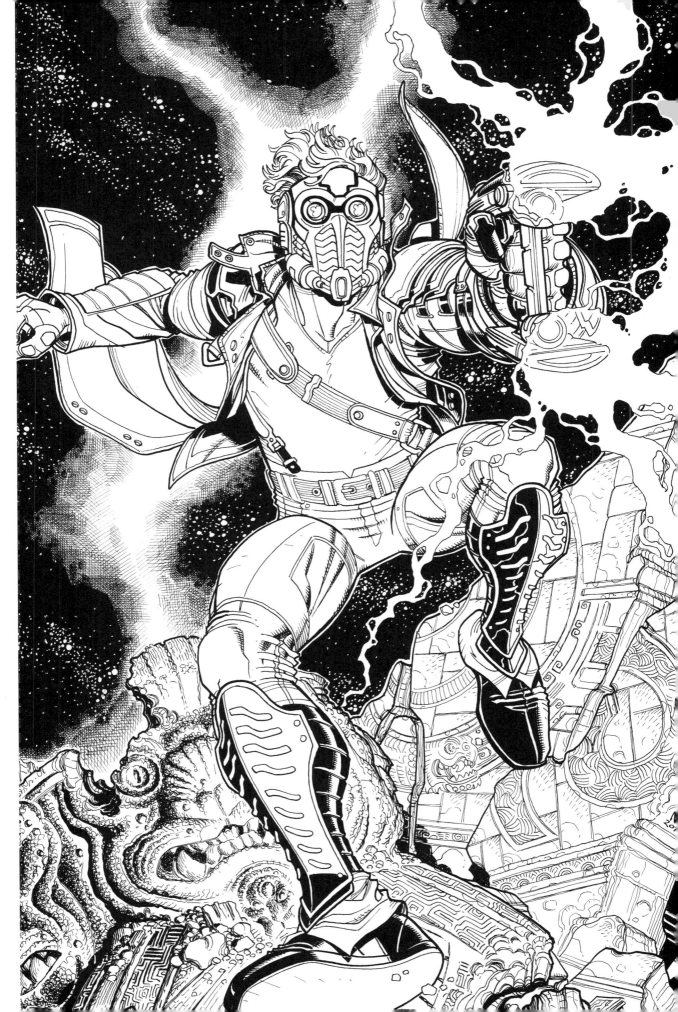

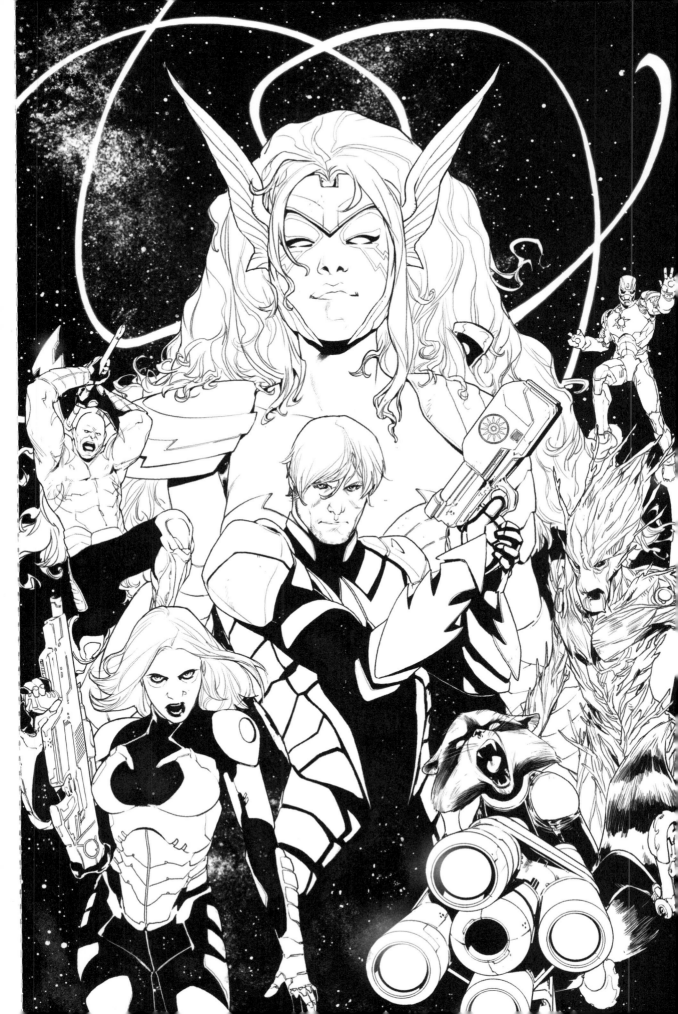

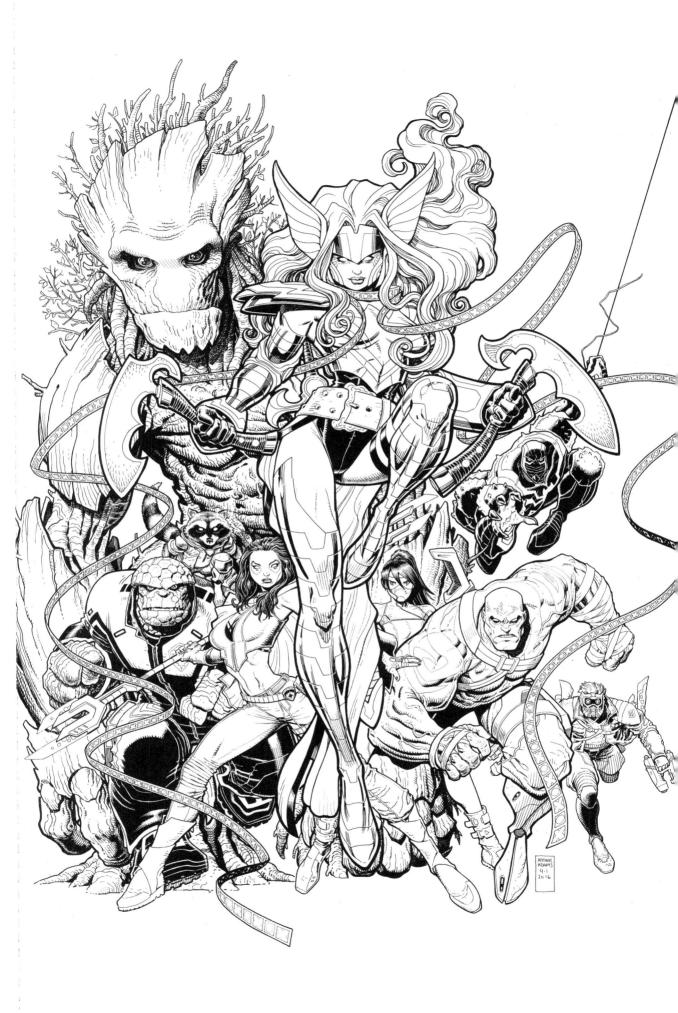

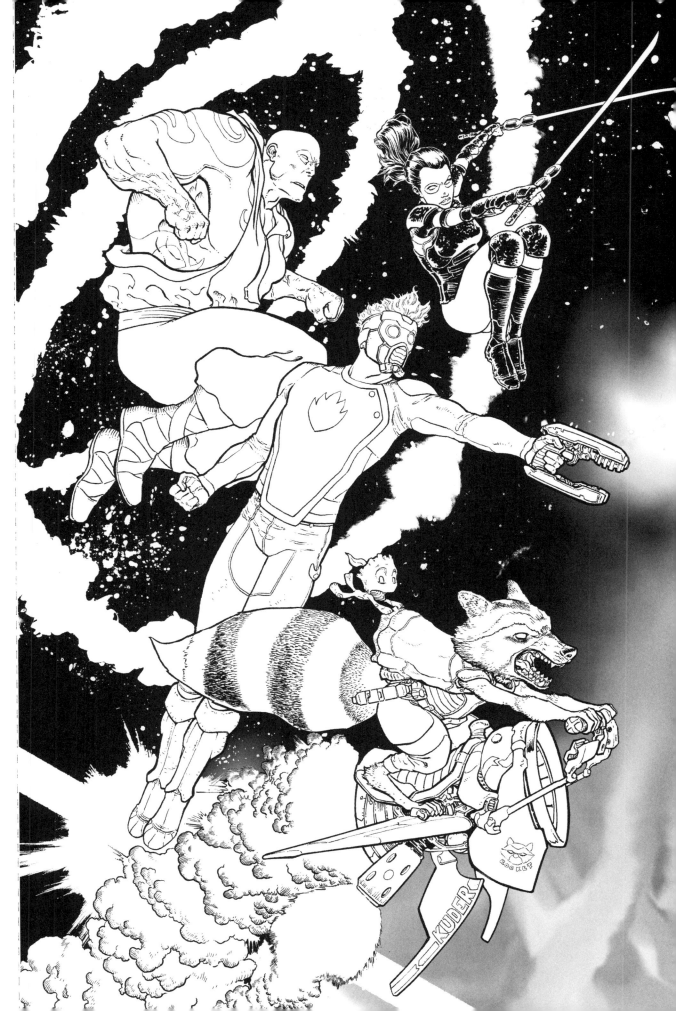

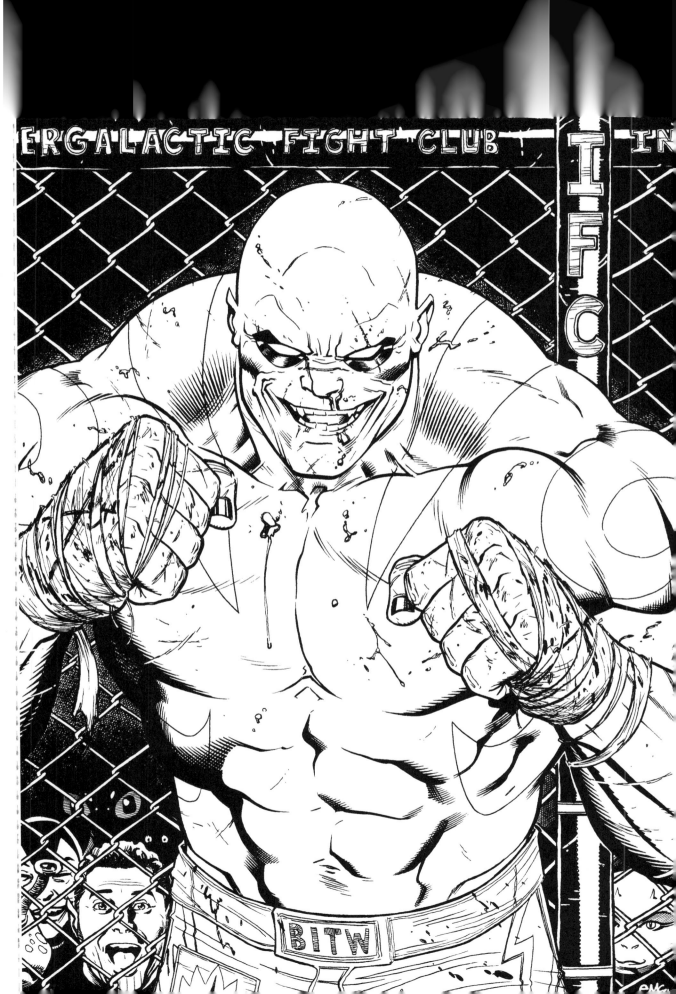

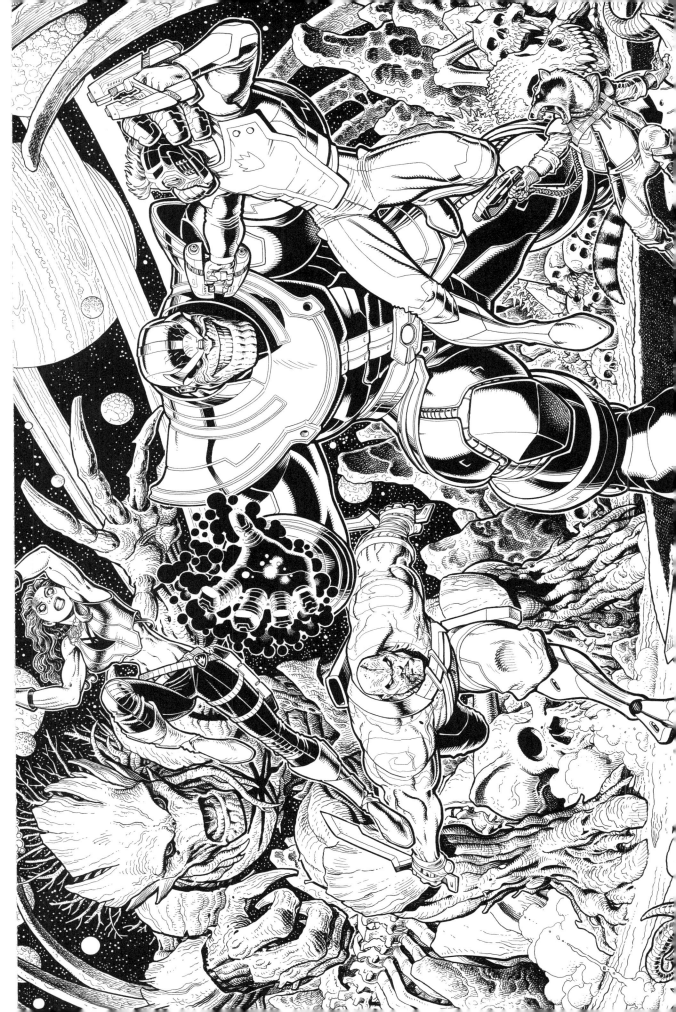

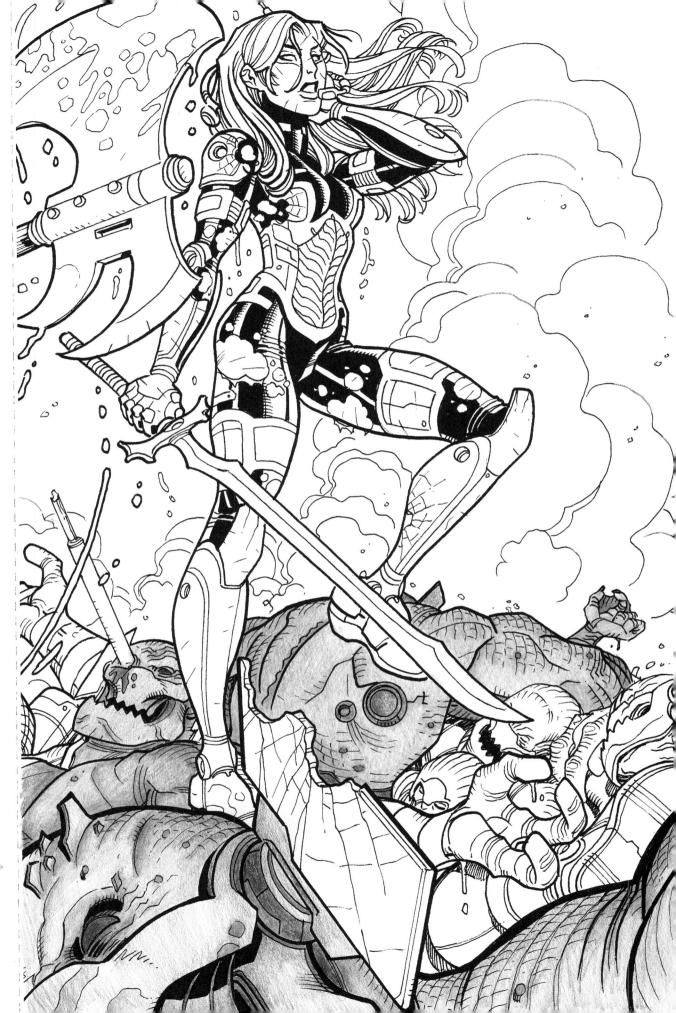

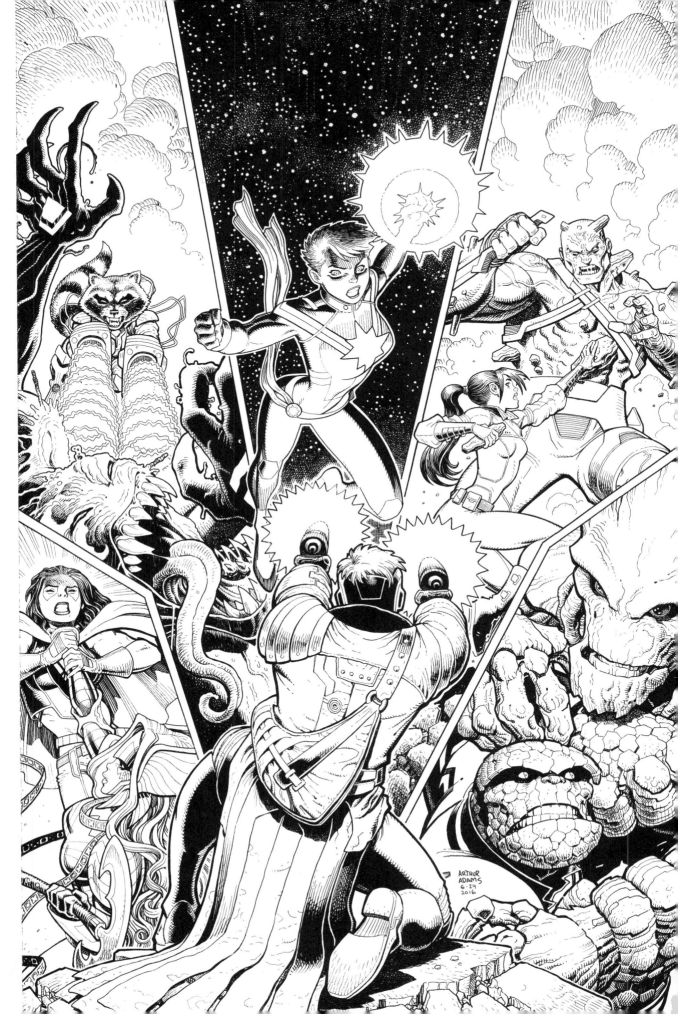

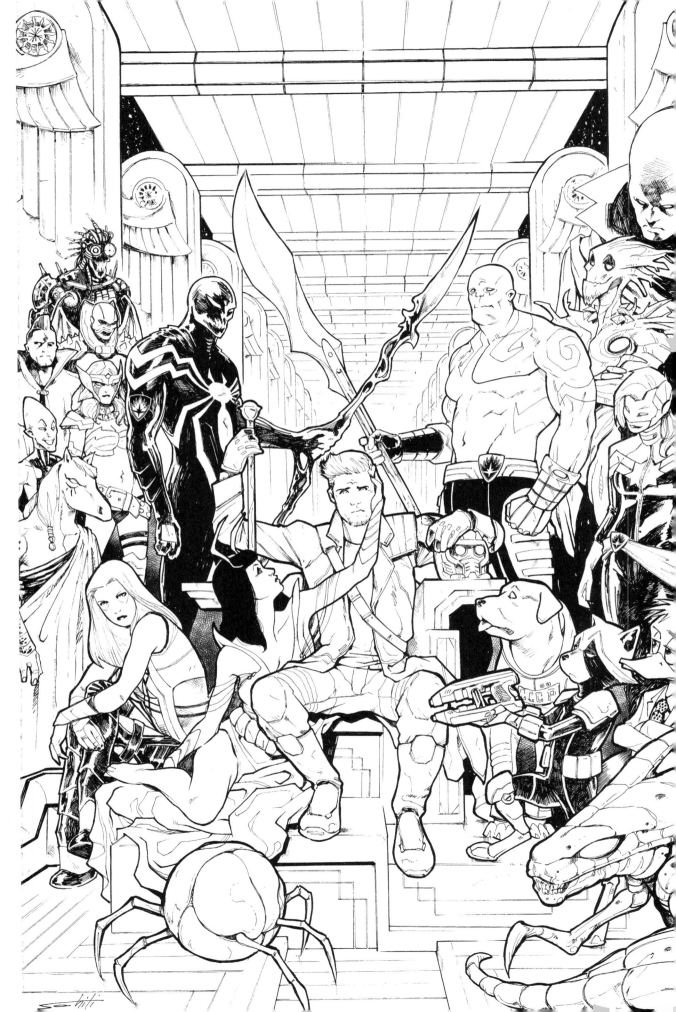

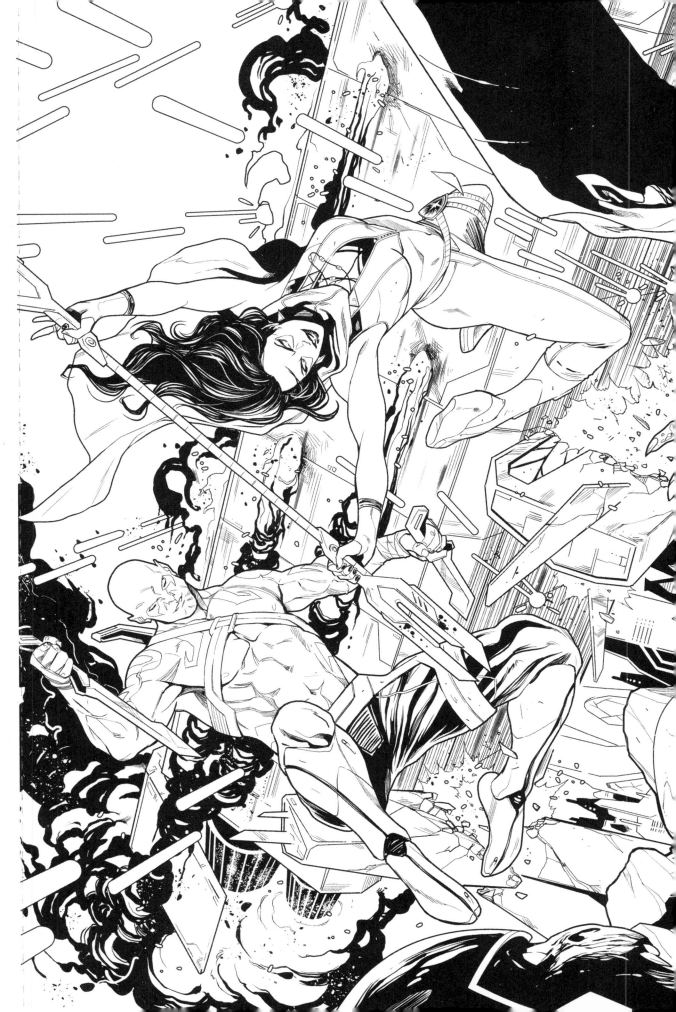

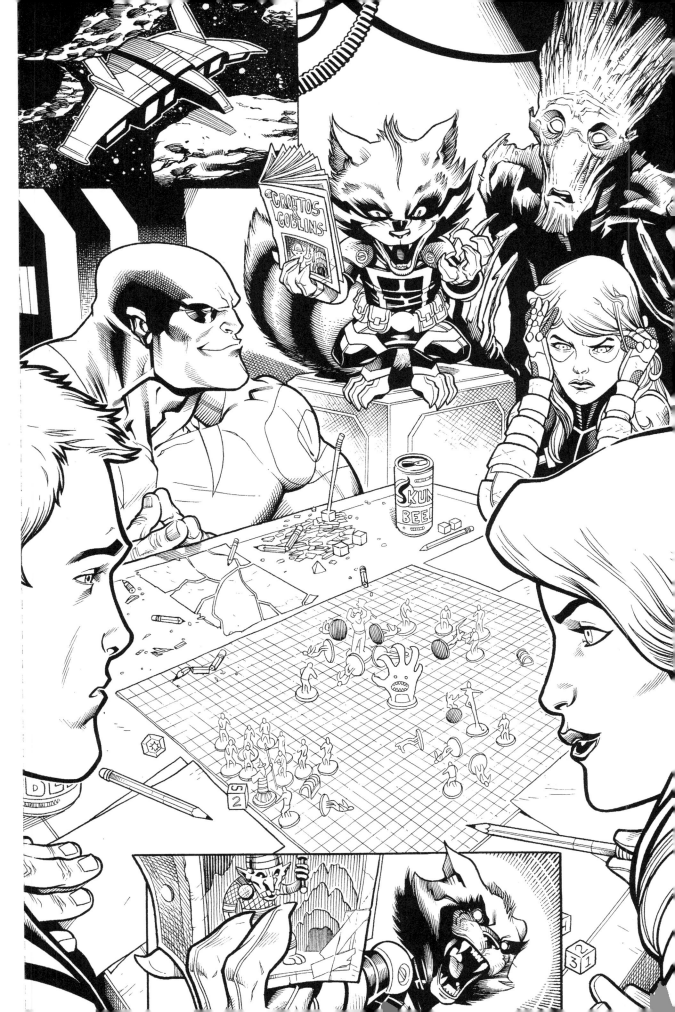

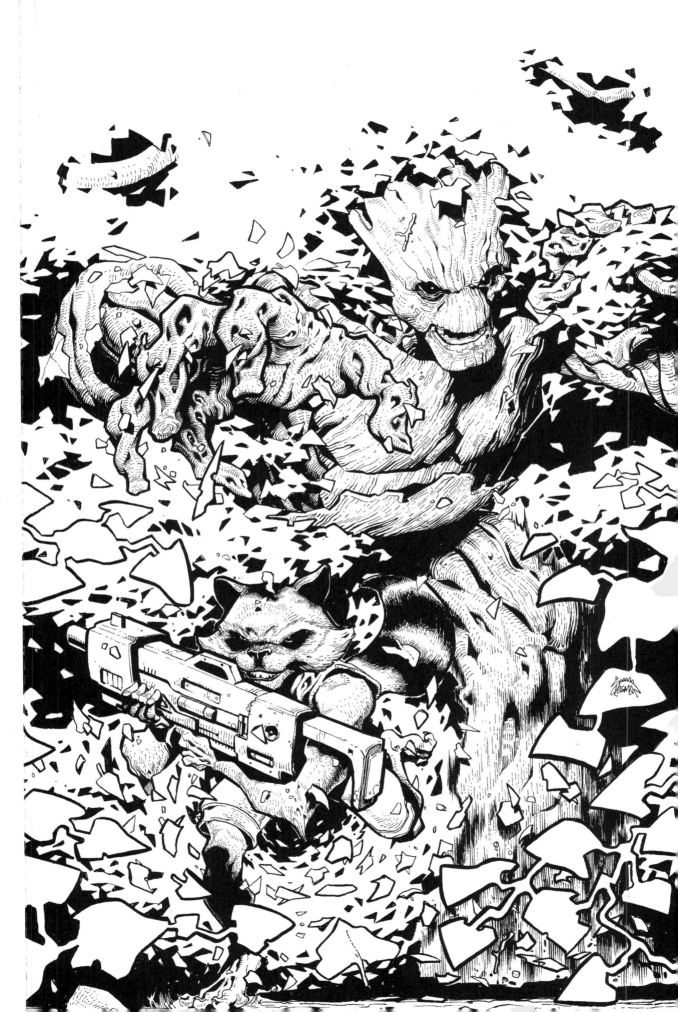

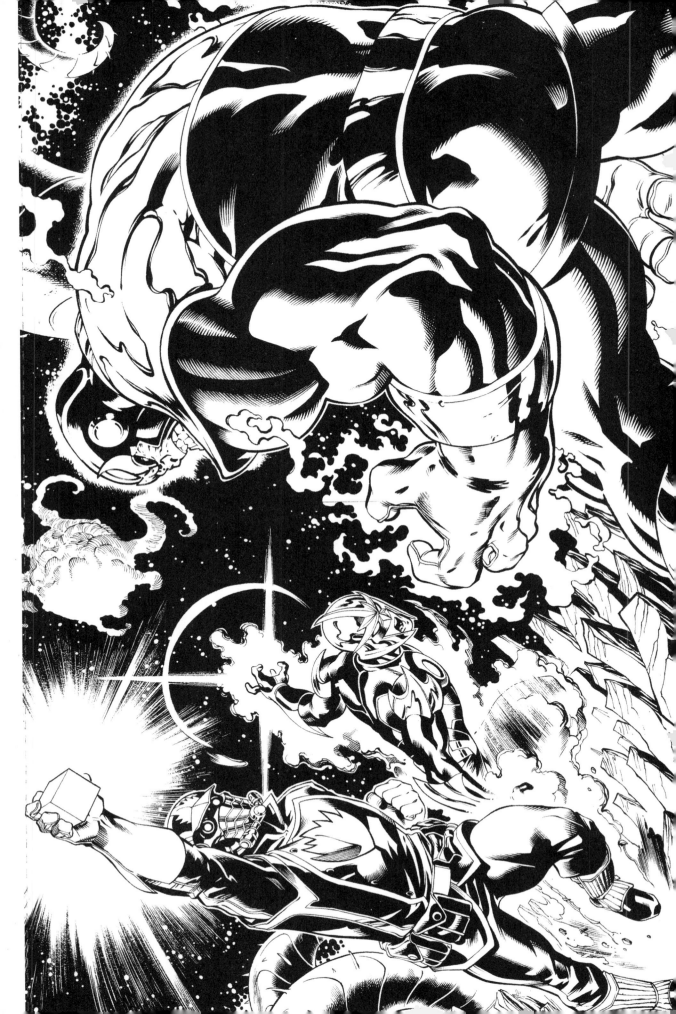

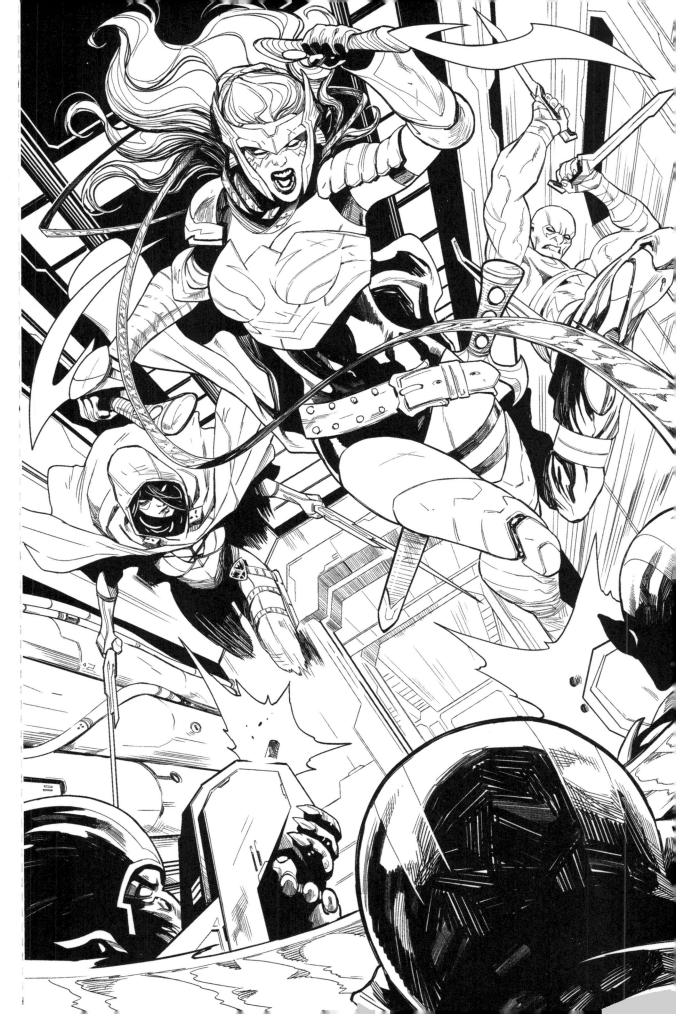

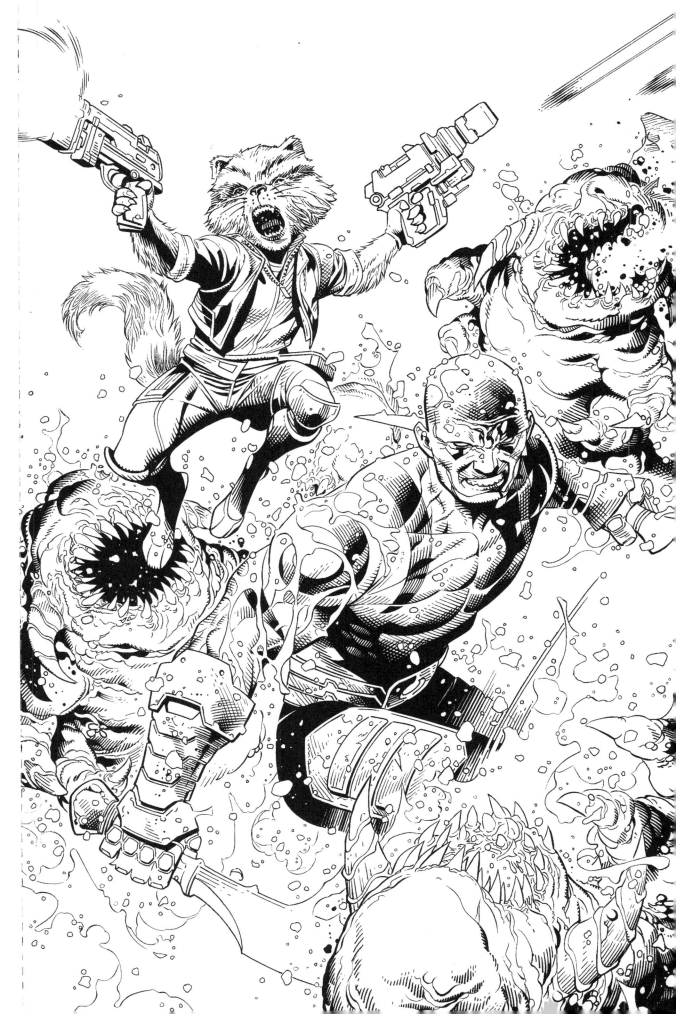

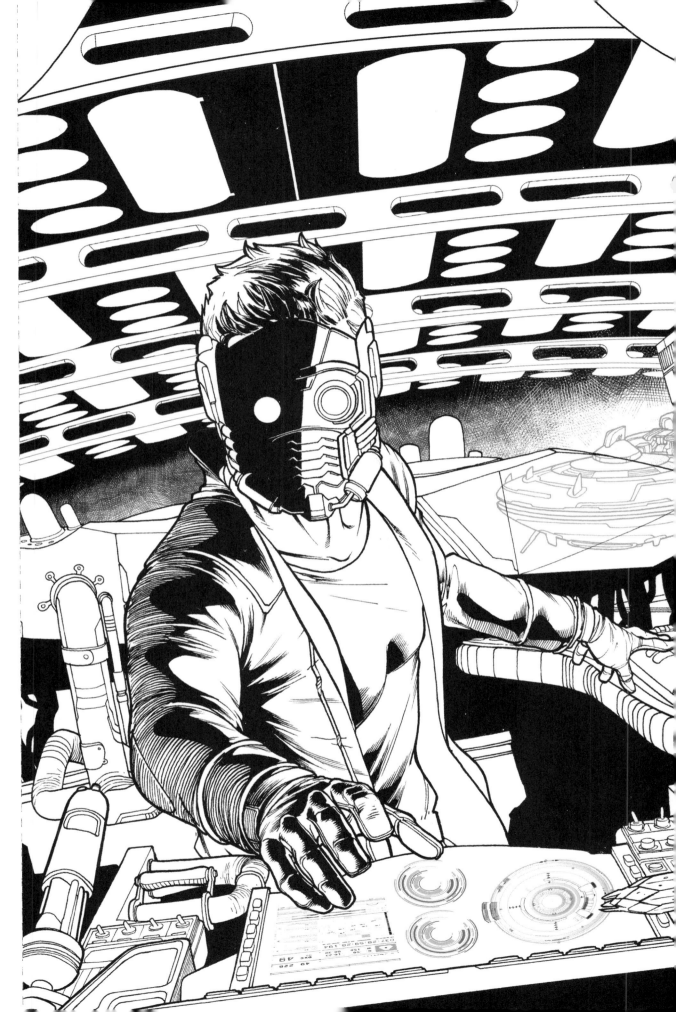

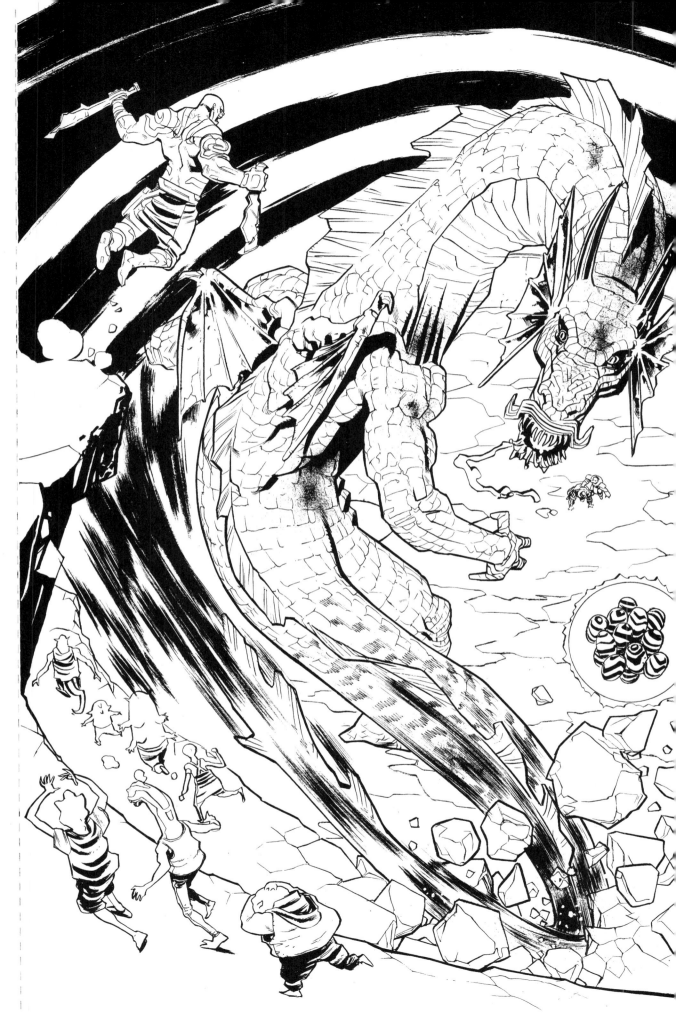

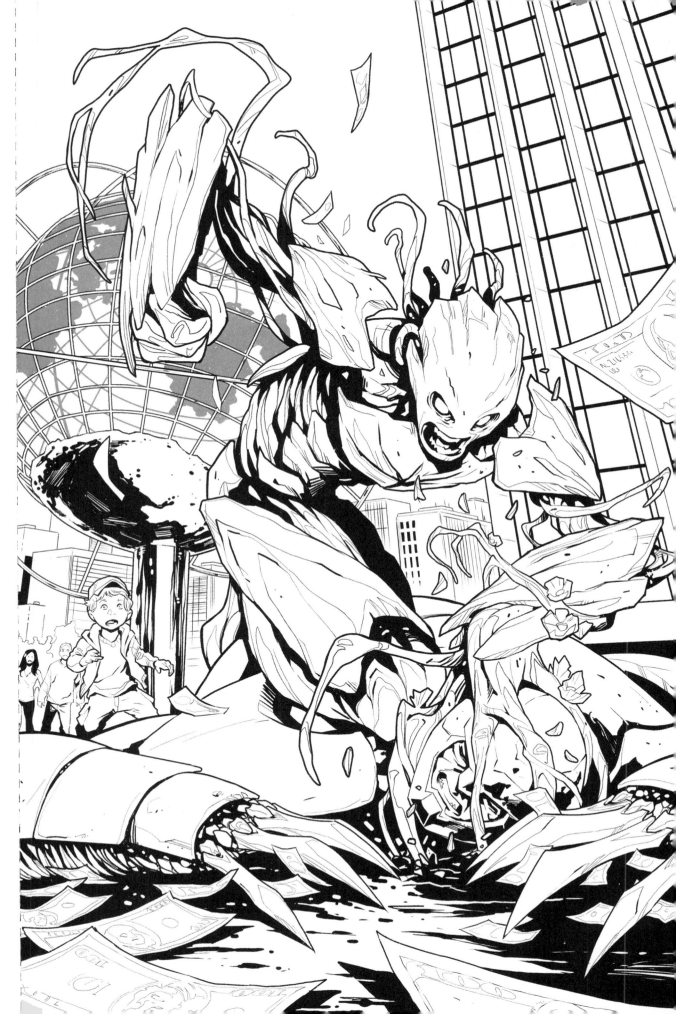

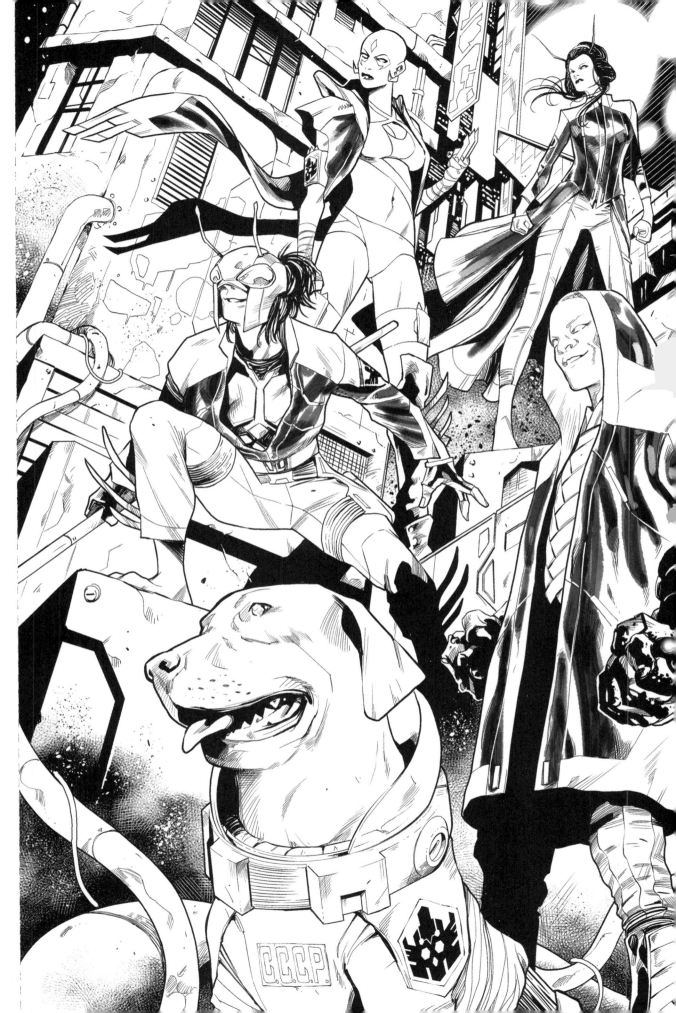

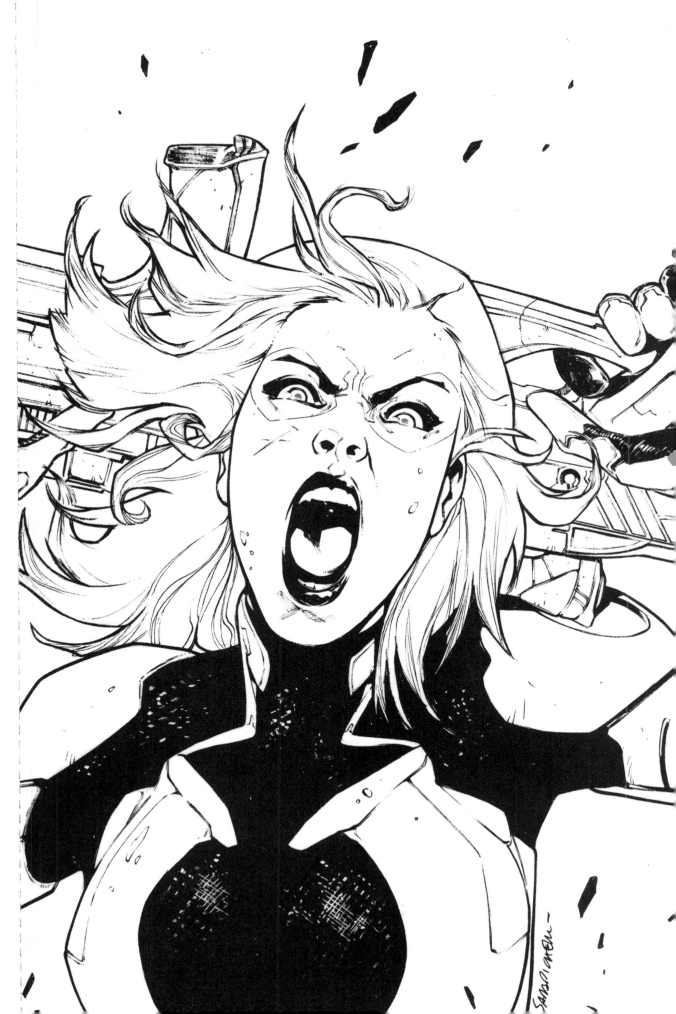

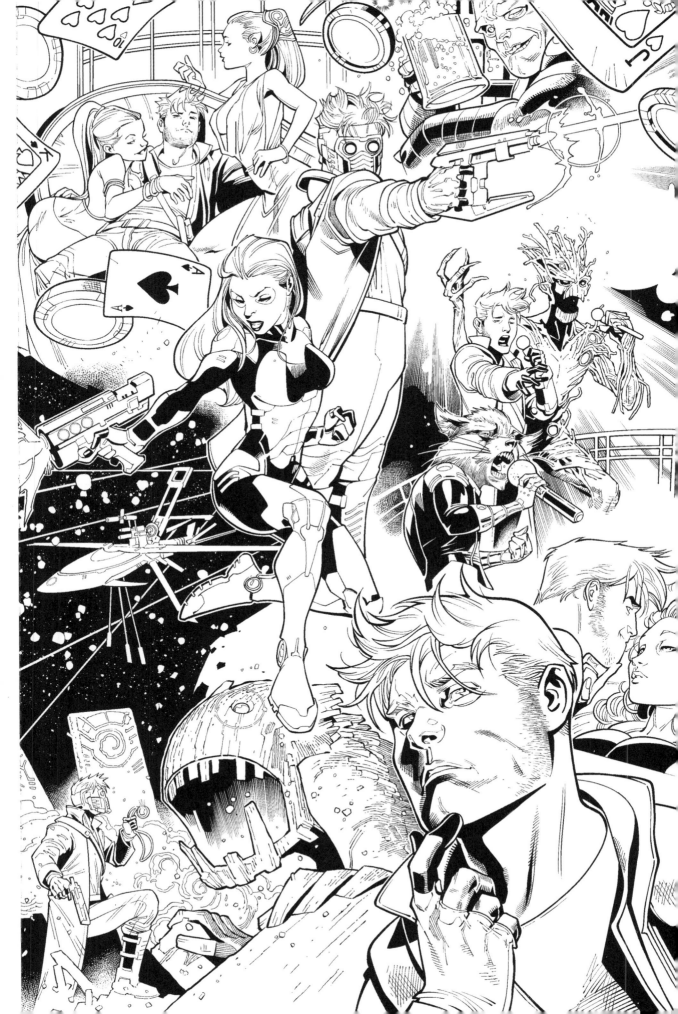

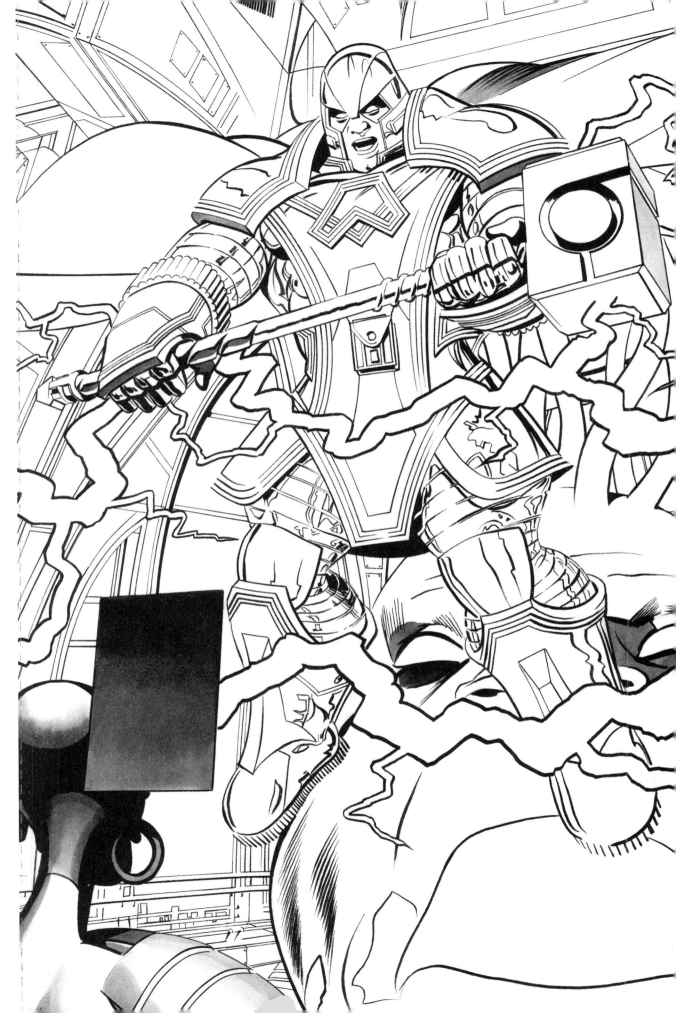

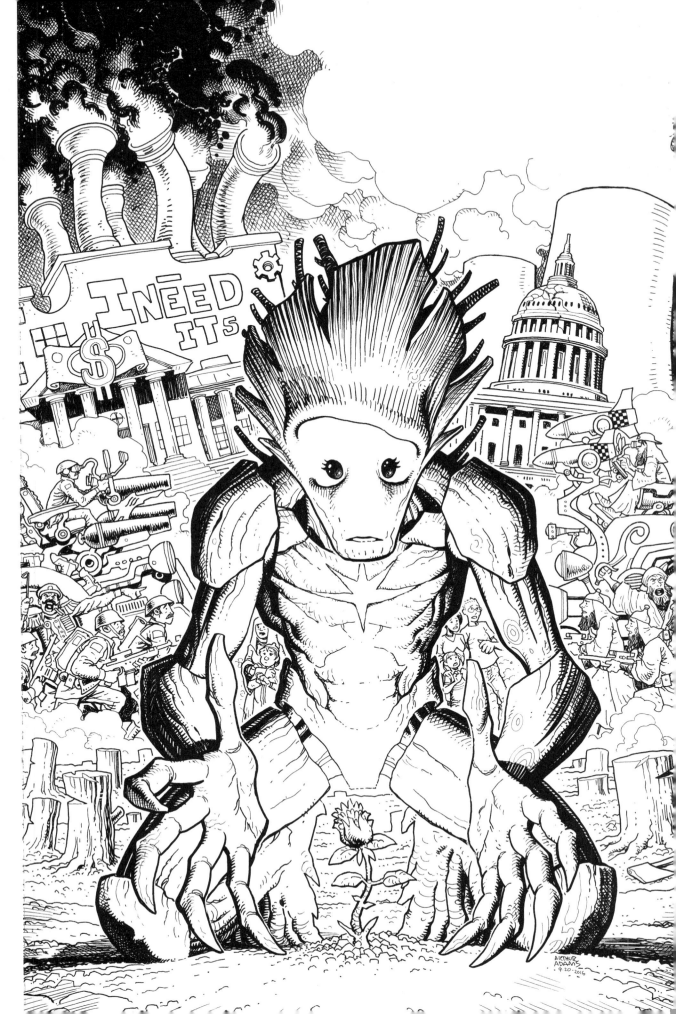

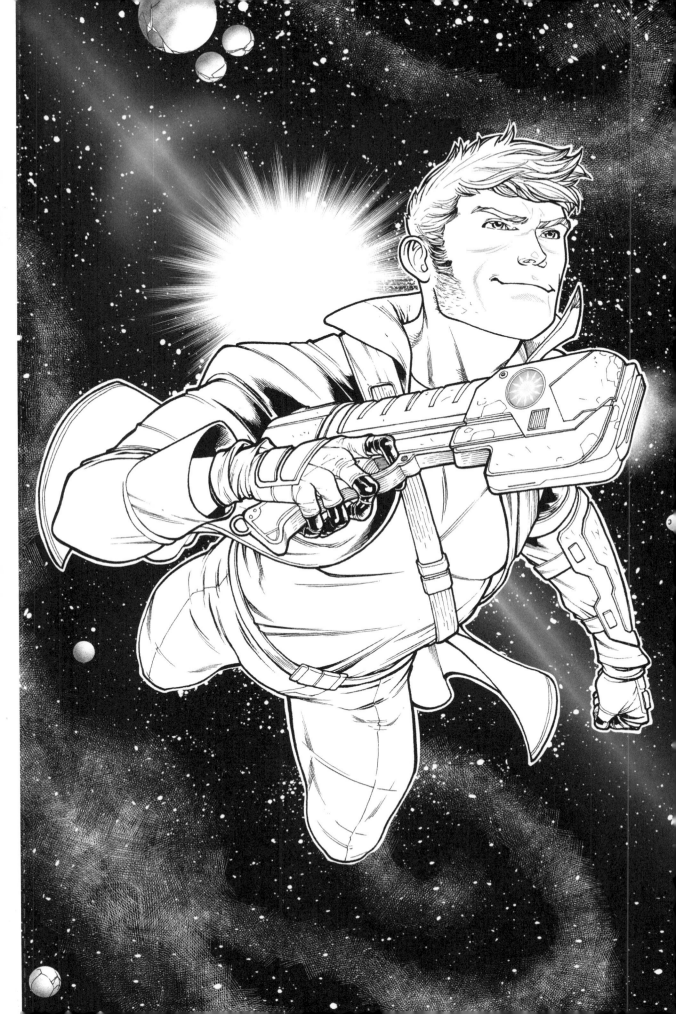

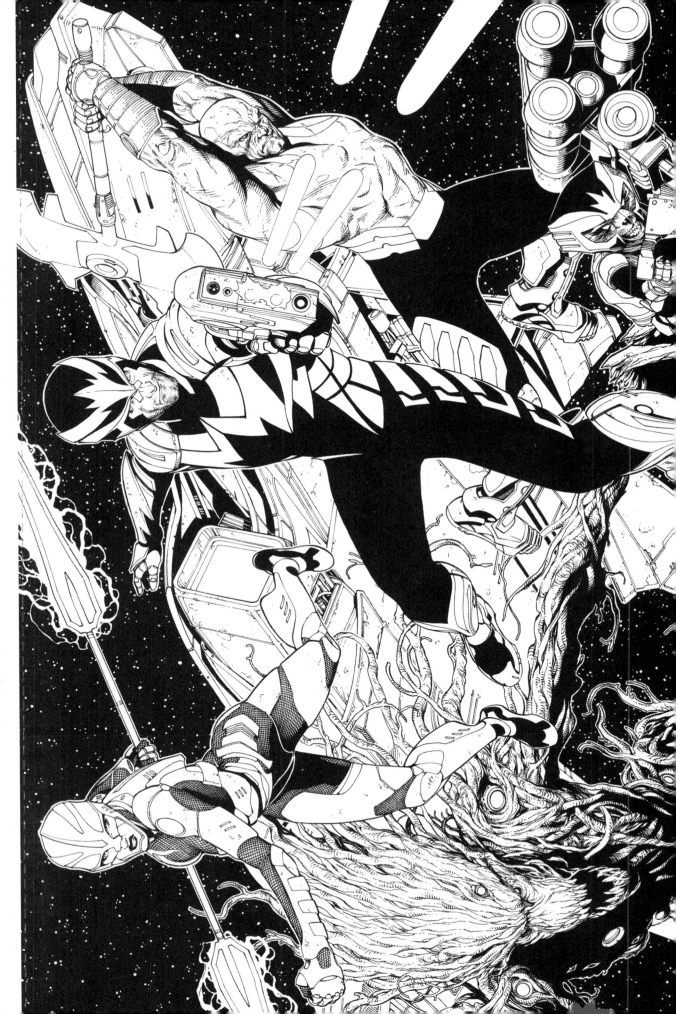

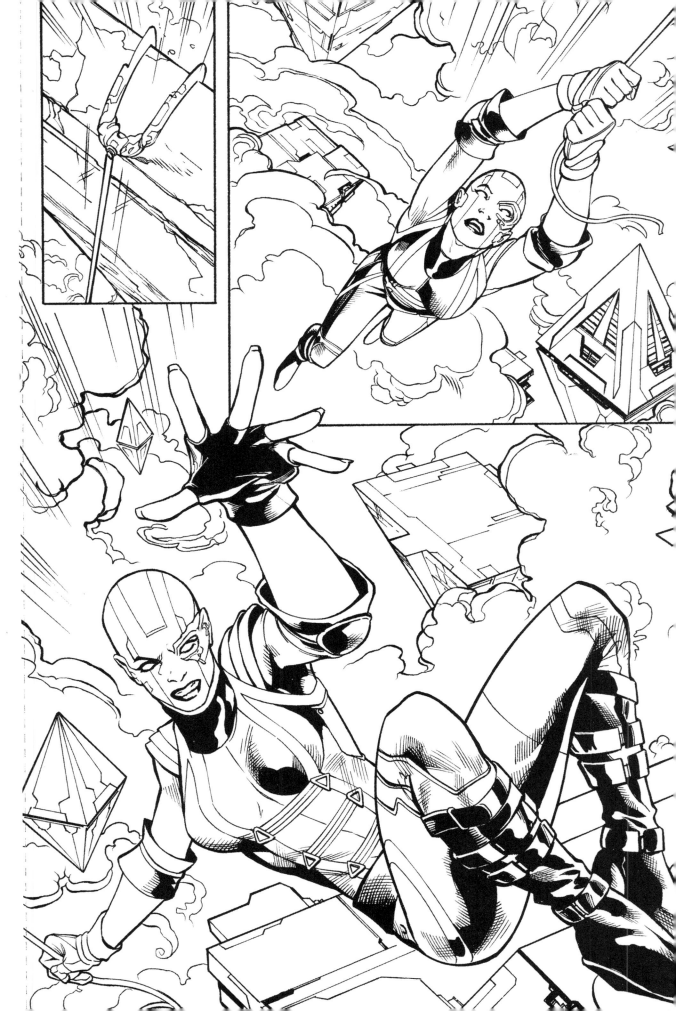

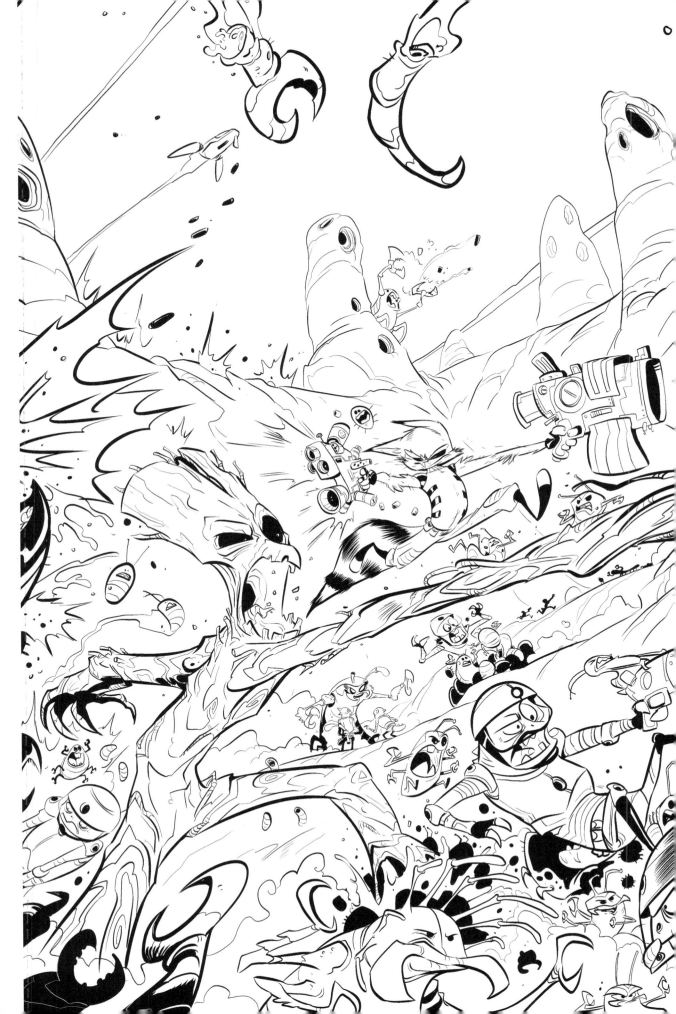

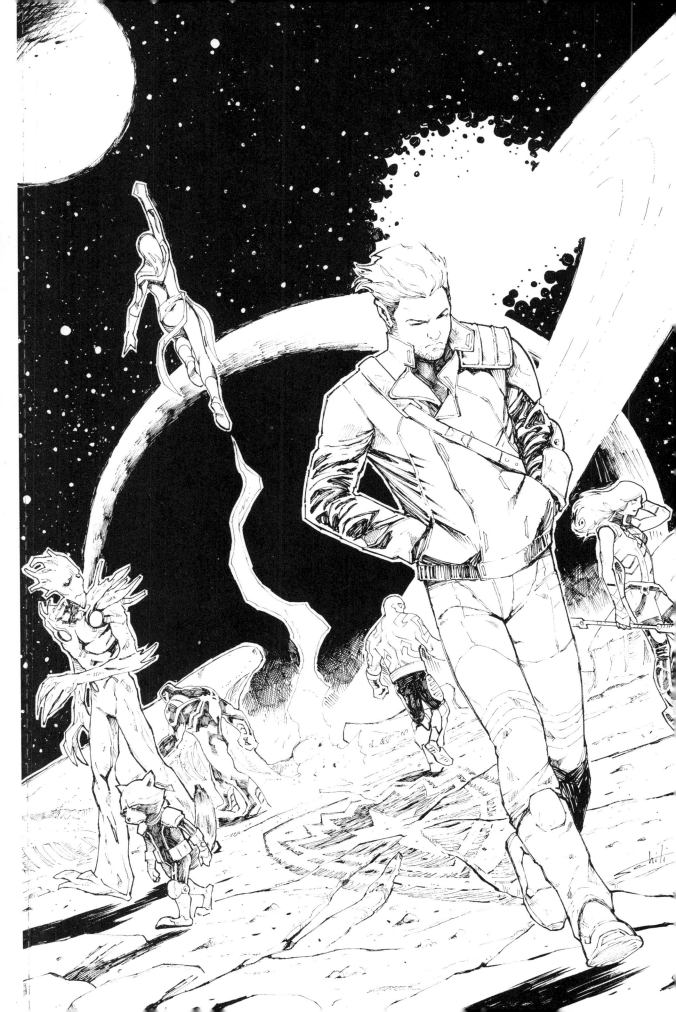

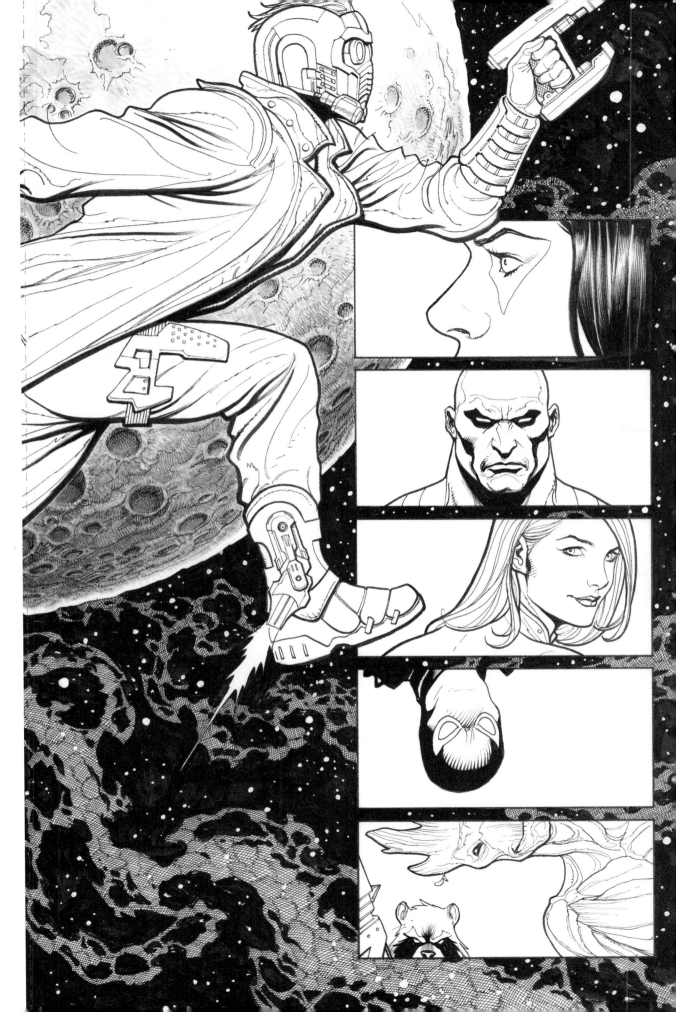

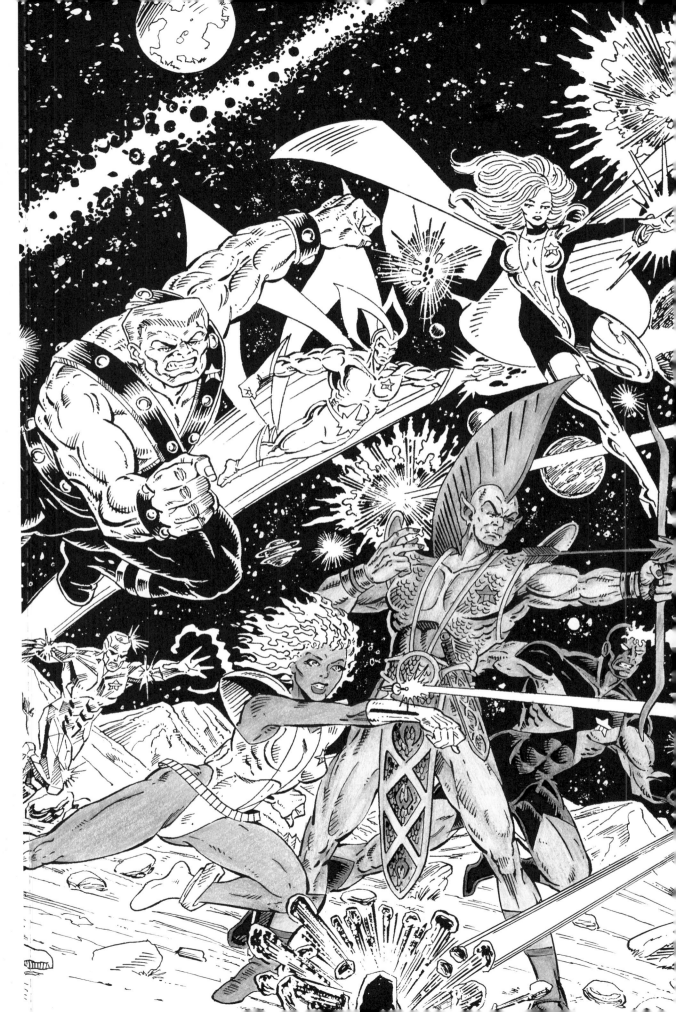

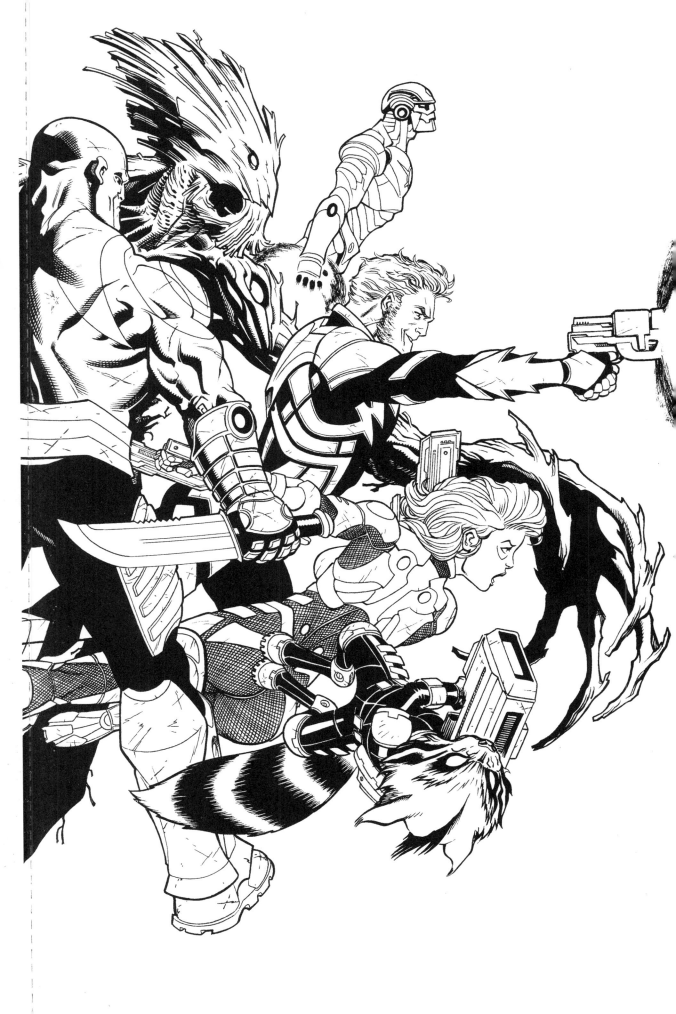

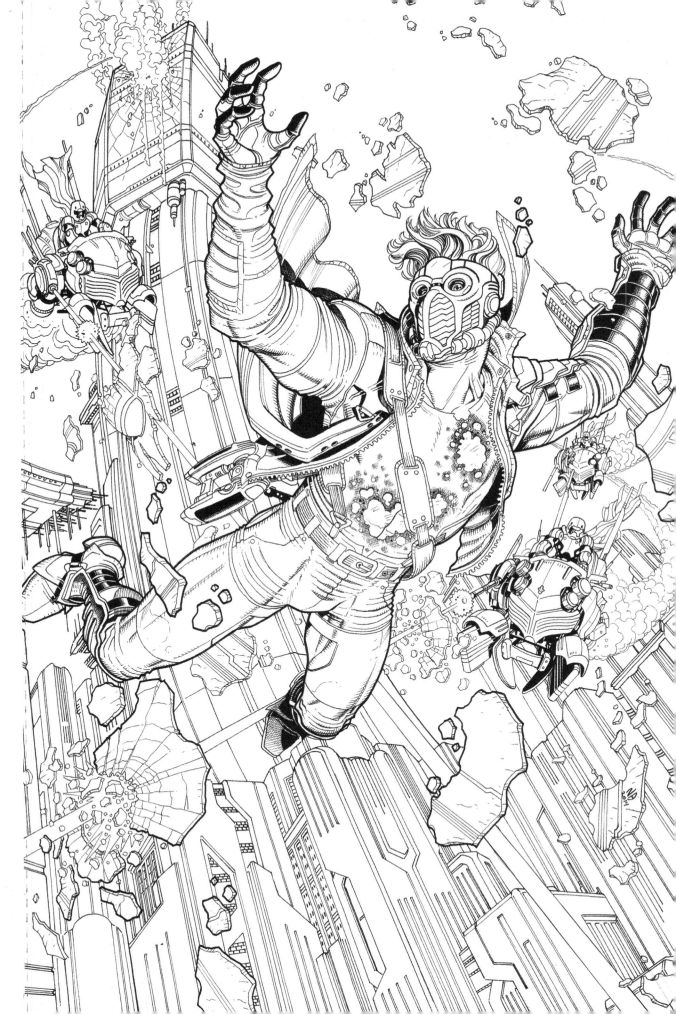

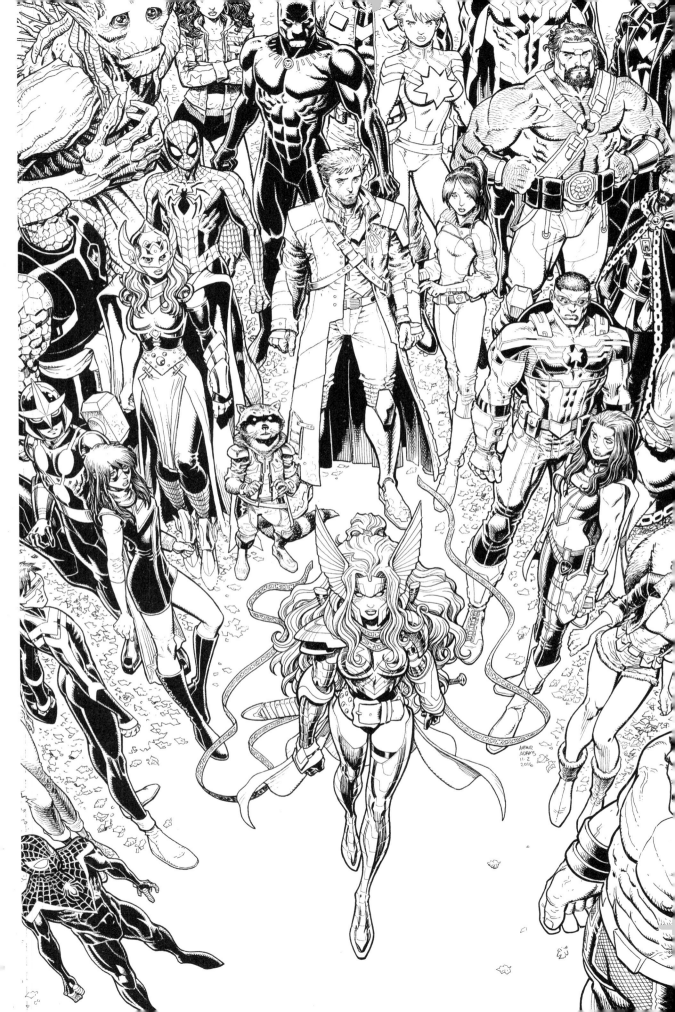

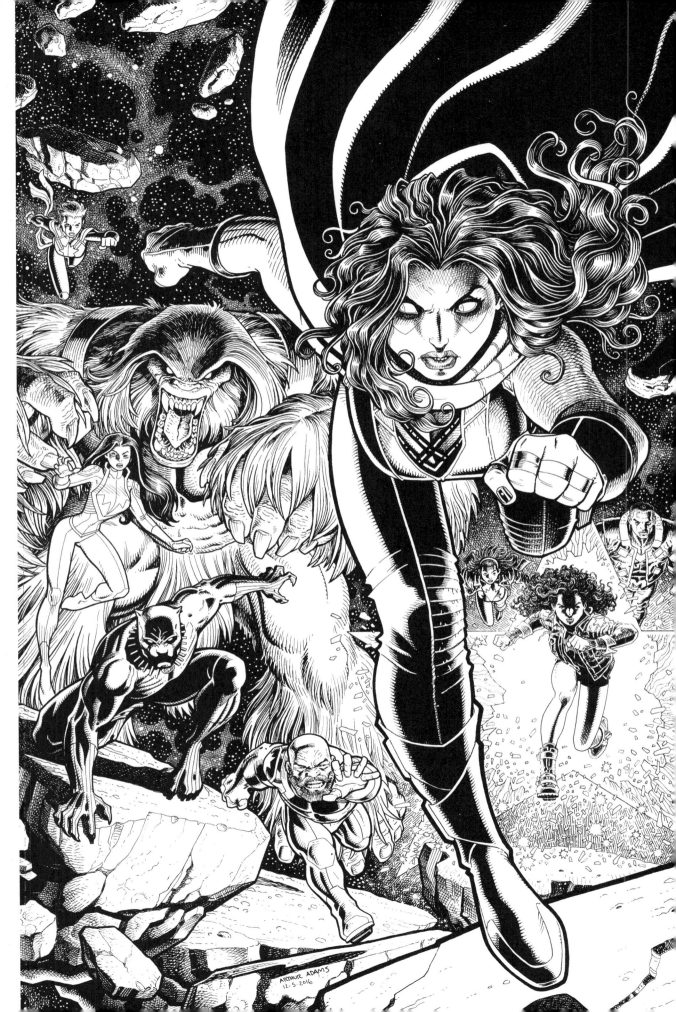

ARTHUR ADAMS
12·5·2016

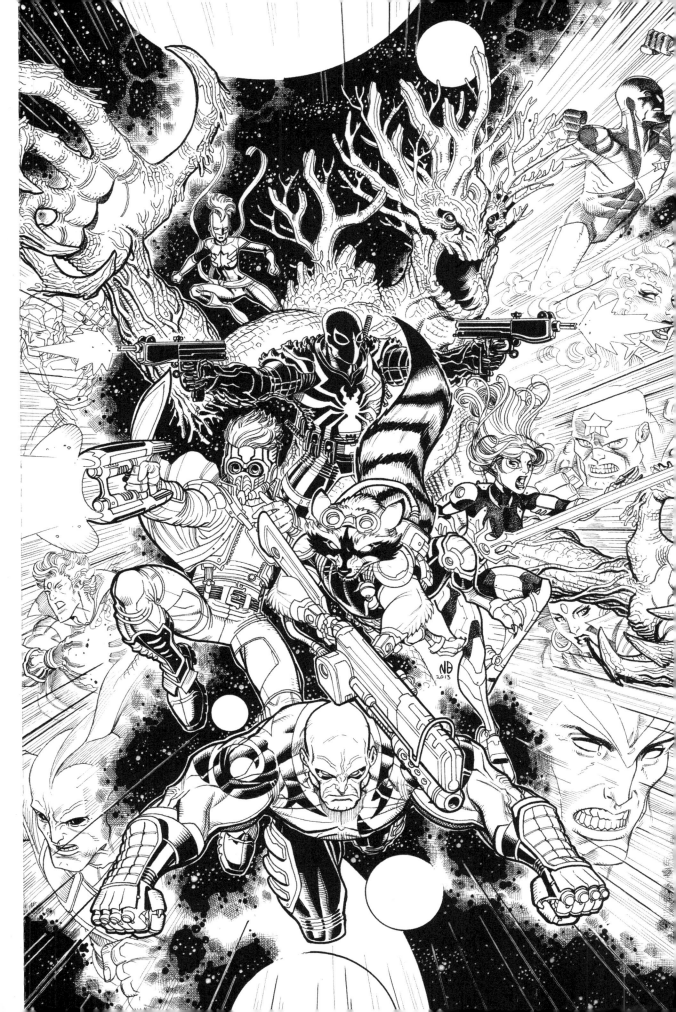

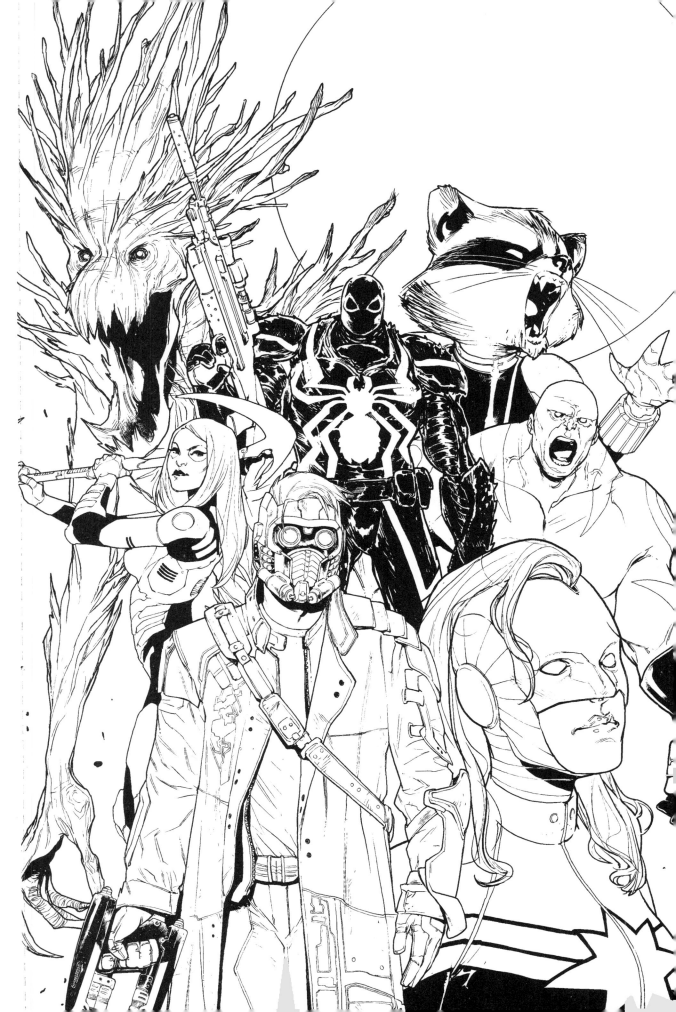

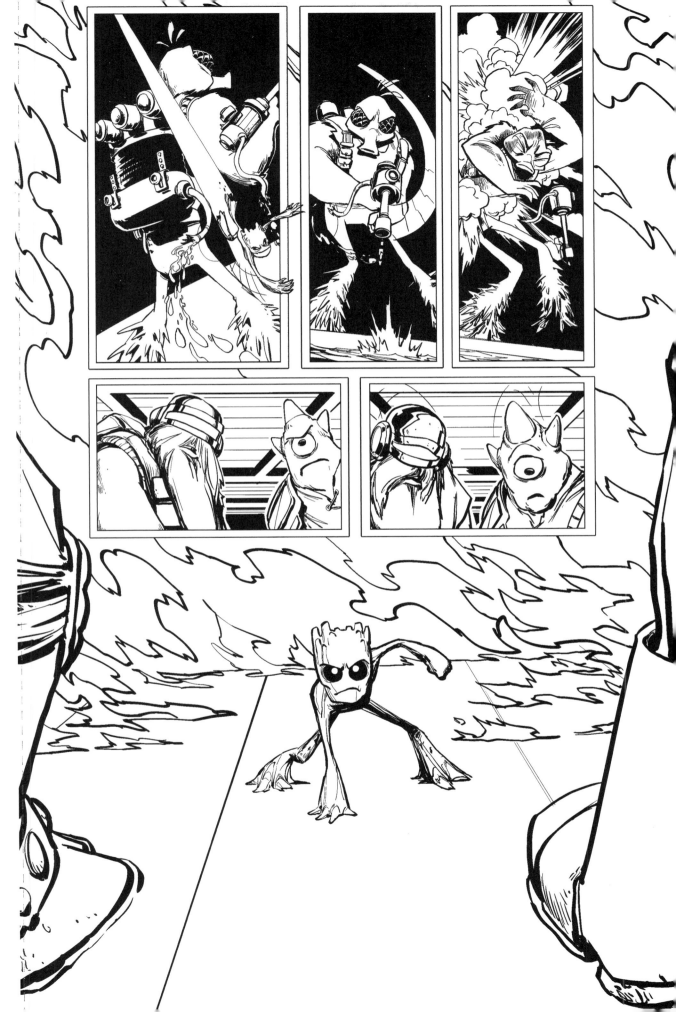

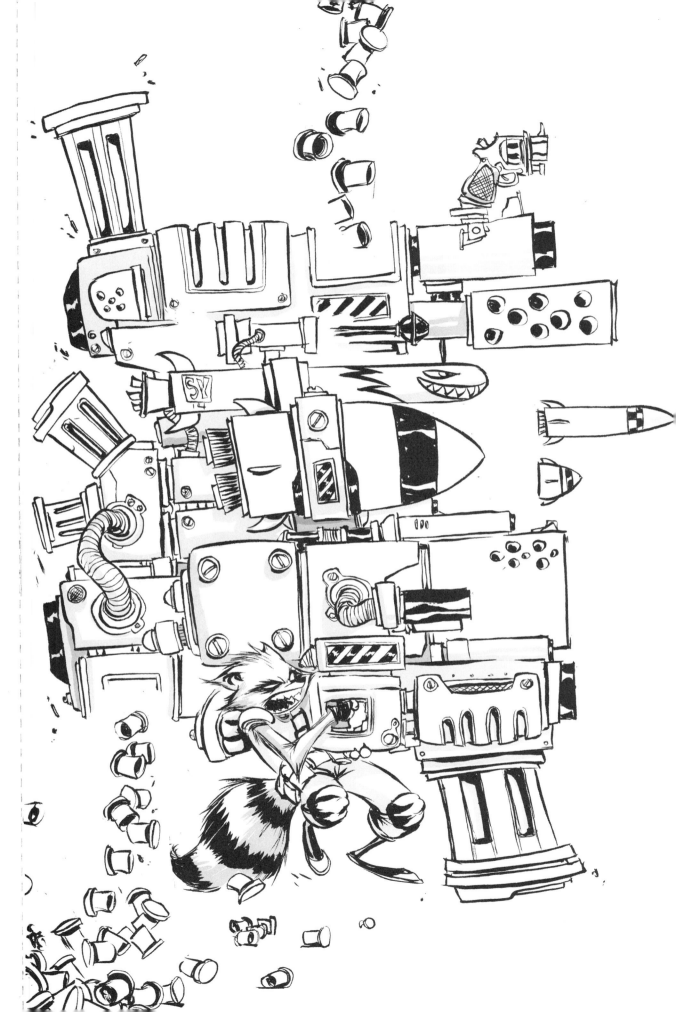

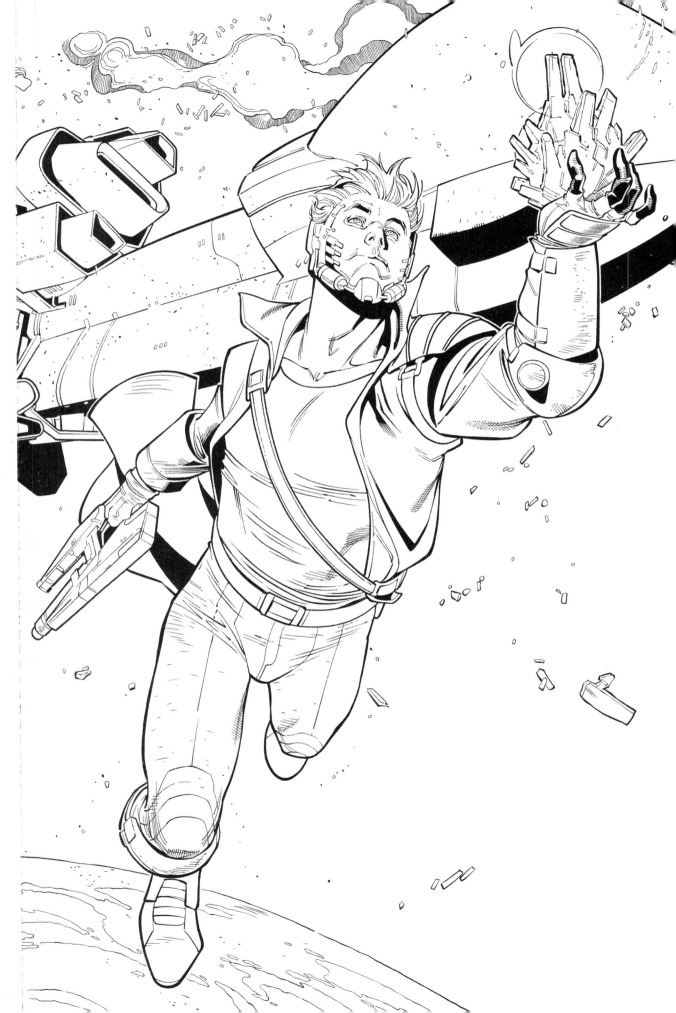

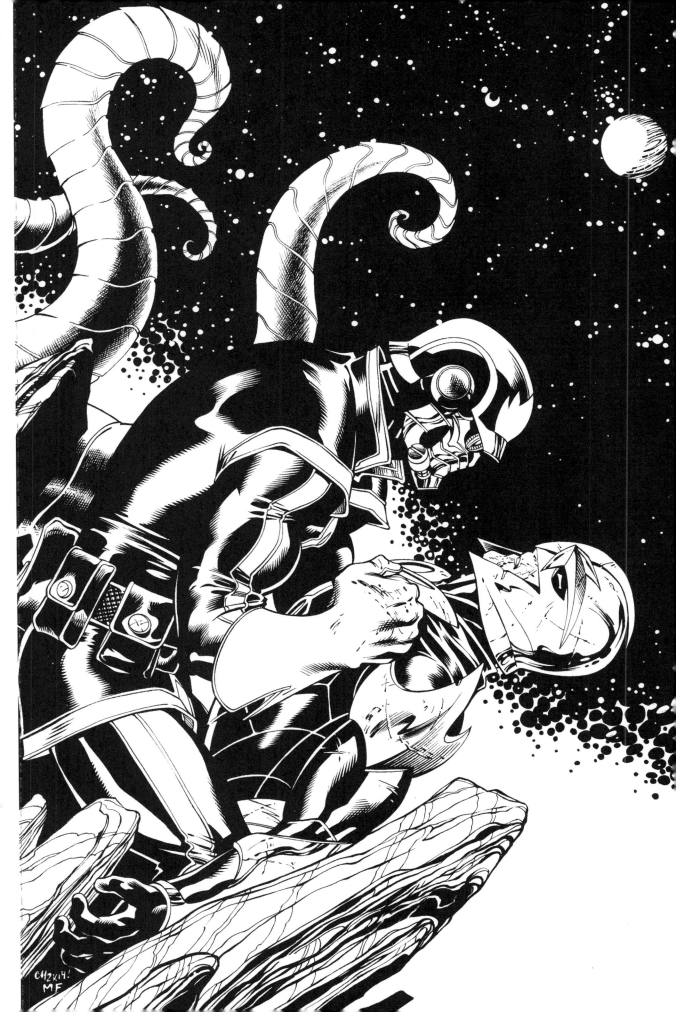

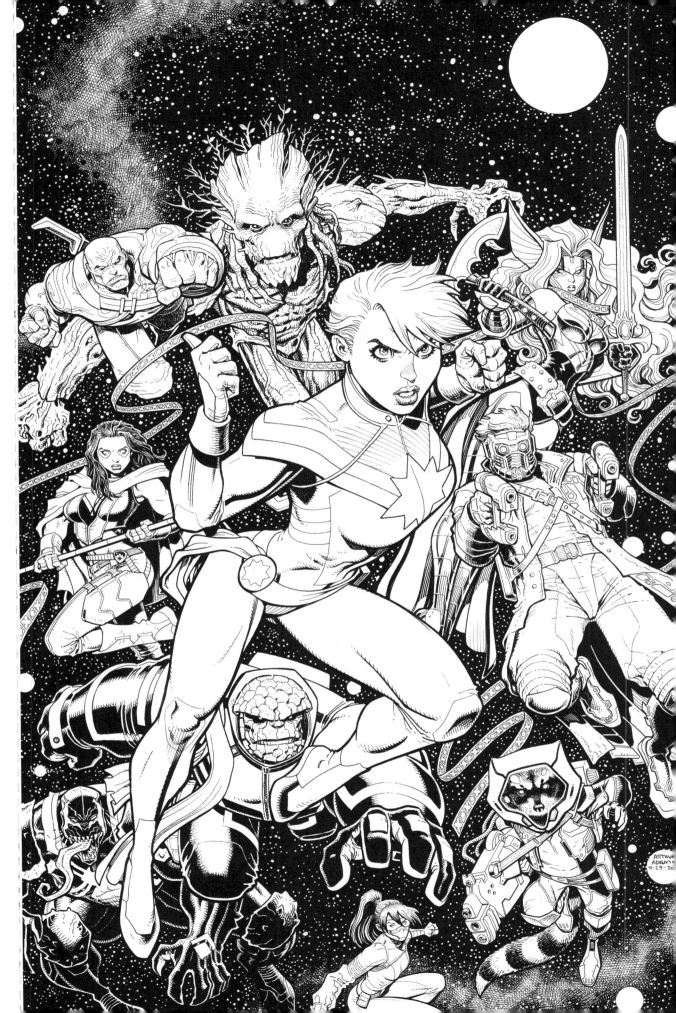